JESUS

THE WORD OF GOD

SERMONS ON THE POWER, CHARACTER, AND
LOVE OF JESUS CHRIST

VOL II

EVANGELIST MARTHA P. DAVIS

JESUS
THE WORD OF GOD

SERMONS ON THE POWER, CHARACTER, AND
LOVE OF JESUS CHRIST

VOL II

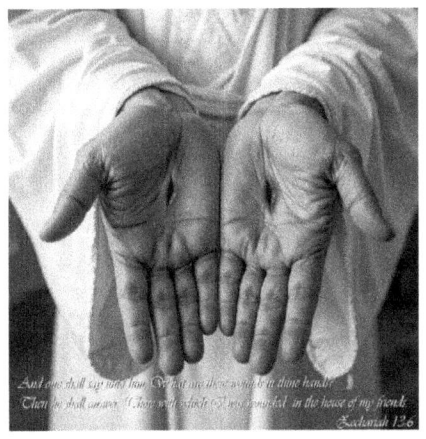

EVANGELIST MARTHA P. DAVIS

ISBN: 978-1-965943-12-0

INDEX

DEDICATION

THIS BOOK IS DEDICATED

TO

GOD THE FATHER

GOD THE SON

AND

GOD, THE HOLY SPIRIT

FOREWORD

It is with deep reverence and joy that we present this powerful collection of sermons, *Jesus the Word of God, Volume Two*, by Evangelist Martha P. Davis. Evangelist Davis was more than a pastor, minister, and evangelist— she was a servant, lover, and friend of the living Christ whose life was wholly surrendered to His will. Every breath she took, every prayer she lifted, and every word she preached bore witness to her unwavering love for Jesus. Her intimacy with the Lord was evident to all who encountered her, and through her ministry she taught others not merely to believe in Him, but to love Him personally, passionately, and intimately.

Her sermons were never just speeches; they were the overflow of a heart ablaze with devotion to Christ. She lived in constant fellowship with Him, and that closeness infused her words with power, tenderness, and authority. Through her preaching, the Holy Spirit moved with undeniable fire—healing the brokenhearted, lifting the weary, restoring faith, and igniting in others the desire to pursue Jesus more deeply. Evangelist Davis carried within her a holy urgency: that all people might come to know the Lord not as a distant figure, but as a living Savior who longs for a relationship with His children.

This volume is far more than a collection of sermons—it is a living testimony of a holy servant who loved Jesus above all else and labored faithfully to draw others into that same love. Though she has gone home to be with the Lord, her words remain anointed and alive, pointing us back to the heart of Christ. As you read these messages, my prayer is that you will feel the presence of Jesus drawing you nearer, filling you with His Spirit, and reminding you that His Word endures forever.

Evangelist Martha P. Davis has finished her race, but her love for Jesus and her passion for His people continue to shine through these pages as a guiding light. May her example inspire you, may her words encourage you, and may her devotion stir within you a deeper longing to know and love Jesus with all your heart.

In Christ's love,

G.K.Montilla

THE BLOOD OF JESUS

First Aired October 1ˢᵗ 1995

Precious Father, in Jesus' name, we come before the mercy seat and the grace of God we obtain by faith in Jesus' name. Thy will be done as we go into the Word, the word of life, the word to enrich us to live more abundantly. Give us thine engrafted word through the knowledge and the power of the Holy Ghost. Give us the revelation power that we have need of, Father. Help us to see Jesus, the purpose for which you sent your Son. Help us to see, help us to know, help us to understand, by the grace that you have given unto us, bless us, thy people.

Help us to hear, help us to understand what you're about to say to us. In Jesus' name, bind the forces of hell that would come to steal, that would come to rob thy word as you give it unto us. Bind him in heaven, we bind him on earth. We lose the spirit of liberty, the spirit of revelation unto the people of God, in Jesus' glorious name, have thine own way. Thy kingdom come, manifest thy glory.

Make it known to the church, the bride of Christ. Hallelujah. Praise your glorious name. Let the anointing of the Holy Spirit be upon us. Word our mouths through the unction of the Holy Ghost. Word our mouths, Father. Sanctify our ears, let our hearts be receptive to your will and to your word. Give us to be hearers that we might be equipped to be doers of your word, that we might have an understanding of what you are saying to us. That we might use it all the days of our lives and not let it slip. In Jesus' mighty name. Bless your sweet name. Give your angels charge in the midst of us to minister on our behalf. Glory to God in the highest. Amen and amen.

Hebrews chapter 9 gives us an understanding of the pattern of the law of Moses. A very clear understanding. My main theme here is to speak of the blood of Jesus Christ. The blood of Jesus Christ. In chapter 9, verse 1,

> *Then verily the first covenant had also ordinances of divine service, and a worldly sanctuary. For there was a tabernacle made; the first, wherein was the candlestick, and the table, and the shewbread; which is called the sanctuary. And after the second veil, the tabernacle which is called the Holiest of all; which had the golden censer, and the ark of the covenant overlaid round about with gold, wherein was the golden pot that had manna, and Aaron's rod that budded, and the tables of the covenant; and over it the cherubims of glory shadowing the mercyseat; of which we cannot now speak particularly.*

> *Now when these things were thus ordained, the priests went always into the first tabernacle, accomplishing the service of God. But into the second went the high priest alone once every year, not without blood, which he offered for himself, and for the errors of the people: the Holy Ghost this signifying, that the way into the holiest of all was not yet made manifest, while as the first tabernacle was yet standing:*

> *which was a figure for the time then present, in which were offered both gifts and sacrifices, that could not make him that did the service perfect,*

That could not make him that did the service perfect…

> *as pertaining to the conscience; which stood only in meats and drinks, and divers washings, and carnal ordinances, imposed on them until the time of reformation.*

> *But Christ being come an high priest of good things to come, by a greater and more perfect tabernacle, not made with hands, that is to say, not of this building; neither by the blood of goats and calves, but by his own blood he entered in once into the holy place, having obtained eternal redemption for us.*

Verse 11 again,

> *But Christ being come an high priest of good things to come, by a greater and more perfect tabernacle, not made with hands, that is to say, not of this building; neither by the blood of goats and calves, but by his own blood he entered in once into the holy place,*

not like the priest that had to go in yearly…

> *He entered in once into the holy place, having obtained eternal redemption for us. For if the blood of bulls and of goats, and the ashes of an heifer sprinkling the unclean, sanctifieth to the purifying of the flesh: how much more shall the blood of Christ, who through the eternal Spirit offered himself without spot to God, purge your conscience from dead works to serve the living God?*

> *And for this cause he is the mediator of the New Testament, that by means of death, for the*

redemption of the transgressions that were under the first testament, they which are called might receive the promise of eternal inheritance. For where a testament is, there must also of necessity be the death of the testator. For a testament is of force after men are dead: otherwise it is of no strength at all while the testator liveth. Whereupon neither the first testament was dedicated without blood.

For when Moses had spoken every precept to all the people according to the law, he took the blood of calves and of goats, with water, and scarlet wool, and hyssop, and sprinkled both the book, and all the people, saying, This is the blood of the testament which God hath enjoined unto you. Moreover he sprinkled with blood both the tabernacle, and all the vessels of the ministry. And almost all things are by the law purged with blood; and without shedding of blood is no remission.

without shedding of blood is no remission…

It was therefore necessary that the patterns of things in the heavens should be purified with these;

With the blood,

but the heavenly things themselves with better sacrifices than these.

heavenly things are always better,

For Christ is not entered into the holy places made with hands, which are the figures of the true; but into heaven itself, now to appear in the presence of God for us: nor yet that he should offer himself often, as the high priest entereth into the holy place

*every year with blood of others; for then must he
often have suffered since the foundation of the
world: but now once in the end of the world hath he
appeared to put away sin by the sacrifice of himself.*

*And as it is appointed unto men once to die, but
after this the judgment: so Christ was once offered
to bear the sins of many; and unto them that look
for him shall he appear the second time without sin
unto salvation.*

Hallelujah, it's a glorious chapter, a glorious chapter giving
us to understand that under Mosaic law, God required it. It
was handed down to Moses by God that there would be
sacrifices of slain animals. Sacrifices of goats and calves,
even turtle doves, amen, of lambs, of rams; they sacrificed
these animals for their blood. Because God required blood
to cleanse.

When you sit at the Lord's feet and you wonder why blood,
why blood? As I said earlier today, God is always giving.
God is the giver of life. He gave Himself, He gave Himself,
and He continues to give us Himself, but not through dying.
Jesus was offered once Jesus offered himself unto God
once, for death. Only once did he offer himself to God for
death, because only once was enough, and it was done. As
we look back to the cross, all of this was pertaining to the
cross. It was looking toward the cross that Moses and
Aaron and the priests, and the high priest did in a ritual,
you might say, every year.

It could not save; it could not purge the conscience from
dead works. This is why it had to be offered yearly, because
men kept sinning, they kept sinning. They were born in sin
and shaped in iniquity. From Adam's fall, from Adam and

5

Eve's fall, brought sin upon all the world, upon all human beings. So whether we were born in sin by our parents' consent, they will that we be born, this is why we are here. But as an infant, we are under the academic law until we come into the knowledge of Jesus Christ.

We need the salvation that only Jesus can offer. Now, when I say under the law, I mean under sin. Every man hath sinned and come short of the glory of God. And no matter how much grace and truth and redemption with the blood of Jesus Christ is present today, man must come to the knowledge that Jesus has paid the price for their sins with his own blood, amen. And the law of Moses gives us to know that we were born in sin. If we had not been born in sin, there would be no reason for the law, but the law could not save us; the blood of goats and calves and heifers and so forth could not redeem us. It was only a pattern of foreshadowing of the true sacrifice, who is Jesus Christ.

And every year under the mosaic law, they had to shed blood; it was required. Why? Because the (animal)blood could not give life, of the goats and the heifers and the rams and whatsoever was used for sacrifice… but Jesus said, prepare me a body, I will redeem man, and he offered himself to God before he came to this world. All of this was done in heaven before Jesus came to this earth.

The Godhead body seeing ahead of time the fall of man and the failure of man, and the rituals that man would do for cleansing. Because man had a conscience and still does, and that conscience was bearing witness to what was right and what is wrong, amen. But man didn't have the remedy, so before Jesus came, God made a way for man to be forgiven yearly of their sins, yearly.

But the Lord God wanted to end that yearly sacrifice that was required. Without the shedding of blood, there is no remission, that means no remission of sin. There is no cleansing from sin without the blood being shed. And then that the goats and heifers and whatever animal sacrifice was given could not finish the work of salvation, it could not redeem man from the fall.

God sent his son from heaven to shed his blood… life for life. Jesus gave his life that we would have life. Why the blood? Life is in the blood. Animals, when they die, they are done; they do not have souls like we do, they are not spirit like we are, their blood was only for then. But Jesus has a soul, Jesus has a spirit, Jesus has a glorified body that was slain, but it lives. It's glorified because the life that was in him, the blood was drained from him, and that blood is yet at work today because it's life.

The blood is life, and our life is in the blood, Jesus' blood that washed us from our sins and yet covers us and keeps us from sin. Just as Jesus died once and has entered into the heavenlies into that sanctuary of the most high God to be our mediator to pray on our behalf. That blood that he has shed for us, that God sees in operation for us today, for every sinner that comes to Jesus Christ, that same blood that was shed almost 2000 years ago, as the Bible says, at the end of the world… is yet in operation, is yet in force, is yet in power today!

And that blood washes, it washes the sin, it washes the stain, and it not only washes it completely purifies. It purifies the mind, it purifies the heart, it purifies the body, the blood that Jesus shed for there's life in his blood. And just as the blood made us alive by cleansing us and made our souls and spirits alive unto God, it quickens us today. The blood quickens us alive, hallelujah!

Now we know the word of God quickens us, we know the spirit of God quickens us, but the blood quickens us alive, and that's why God requires that we stay under the blood, that we live in the blood. You hear people say, I say it myself many times, Lord keep us dripping wet with the blood of Jesus. The blood is not only our salvation, it's our covering, the blood protects us from sin, amen. But we have to be conscious, we have to be conscious of the blood amen. That the blood works, it's at work, and it continues to work.

The word of God tells us that there are three that bear record in the earth, the water, the blood, the blood! The water that Jesus shed out of his body when that spear, that long piercing thing, was thrust in his side, water and blood came out. There's life in water, but the blood is more powerful. But they're bearing record, they bear record today, they're witnessing, bearing record means witnessing, to what God did for us back at Calvary. So when we see Calvary, we see the great sacrifice that Jesus wrought for us that we might have life and that more abundantly.

This is why God will not let us get away with "I'm sorry, Lord, but I'm only human." The blood of Jesus made us more than human! The blood made us royal! We are God's inheritance; the things of the earth could not redeem us, the animals of the earth could not redeem us. So God sent his son to redeem us from guile, from corruption, from sin, from spots, from blemishes. The blood, Jesus' blood, it was not Mary's blood; it was God the Father's blood running through the veins of his son Jesus. And that blood is in force today, in greater force because it was shed for us.

Remember, the writer of Hebrews said it's in greater force, for it has no strength unless the testator dies. Jesus died and he rose again, he rose again, Jesus is alive in heaven in his glorified body, but the blood, the blood was shed for all humanity.

All humanity will not accept the blood sacrifice, but we who have accepted what Jesus has accomplished for us… we have life. We are alive in him; the blood atonement has delivered us from Adam's law, from the Moses law. Adam's law… sin, Moses' law… sacrifice. And here we are, redeemed by the blood of the lamb, the lamb that came from on high. And that's why God requires so much from us today. Because we have a greater way than Adam and Moses, we have Jesus, we have his blood, and it's in force because Jesus gave it up!

Every ounce of blood, he did not say it is finished, till every drop of blood and water was drained. And with the little bit of life that was left and was ebbing out of his mortal body, he said to the Father, "It is finished." Last drop, he gave up the spirit of life in him, for you, for me, for generations before him, generations after him. The blood of Jesus is a greater way, a greater way, a greater way… a greater sacrifice!

Jesus is that sacrifice, that precious blood. This is why we cannot take it lightly; we cannot take the blood of Jesus lightly, amen. Because there is life in the blood, there is deliverance through the blood, hallelujah. Isn't this glorious? It's so glorious, so wonderful, so marvelous what the Lord hath done for us. In Ephesians, the second chapter of Ephesians, an epistle of Paul beginning at the 13th verse,

> *but now in Christ Jesus ye who sometimes were far off are made nigh by the blood of Christ.*

let's read it again, Ephesians 2 verse 13,

> *but now in Christ Jesus ye who sometimes were far off*

far off from God,

> *are made nigh by the blood of Christ.*

So you see the necessity of knowing and understanding why the blood had to be shed. That's how we are brought nigh to God

> *For he is our peace, who hath made both one, and hath broken down the middle wall of partition between us; having abolished in his flesh the enmity, even the law of commandments contained in ordinances; for to make in himself of twain one new man, so making peace;*

It's no more "well this is my thing and that's God's thing" … he made us one, making peace.

> *and that he might reconcile both unto God in one body by the cross,*

by the cross, keep your eyes looking at the cross, and the work that was accomplished there.

> *having slain the enmity thereby:*

having slain the enmity… why did the father require a blood sacrifice? The penalty for sin is death. We all were sinners, we were sinners, sold under sin, shaped in iniquity, and worse than that, we could not help ourselves because it was in our nature to sin. We were void of God. Man did not know God. The penalty for sin is death.

The Bible states that all have sinned and come short of the glory of God. The only redemption for sinful man or restoration from death was through the blood atonement. Atonement means at-one-ment. Atonement, at one with God, or one with God, at-one-ment. The bringing together of two who have been enemies into a relationship of peace and friendship. That was the blood atonement. That was the purpose of Jesus shedding his blood, not only to wash us from our sin and give us life from death, but to bring together two who have been enemies. See... enmity, we were at enmity with God, we were enemies. Can you understand that?

Every sinner is an enemy of God. Even now, even though the way is made for them to become a friend of God through the blood of Jesus Christ, this is why you see haters of God. They're enemies of God. The word of God says they're enemies of the cross of Jesus Christ. Amen. The bringing together of two who have been enemies into a relationship of peace and friendship. That's what the blood atonement attained. Amen.

Not only cleansing us. This is why Jesus said, I do not call you servants, but friends. Now he's speaking all of these things beforehand because he knew that the work would be accomplished. The real work that he was sent to do would be accomplished. He came for that purpose and that purpose only to give his life for us. Life, that we might live because we were dead. When the conscience is not awake unto God, when the soul and spirit are bound in darkness, that's death...death!

This is why you see people walking around dead in trespasses and sins. They're dead while they're still breathing because they are not awake unto God. This is why you see so much sin, because man is alive to evil, but they are dead to good. God is good. And as I said, when time is finished, when time is up, because time will end... eternity still goes on and God will still be good. His mercy endures forever. That means throughout all eternity, to have no end. Amen.

So, without the shedding of blood, there is no remission.

> *For he is our peace, who hath made both one, and hath broken down the middle wall of partition between us;*

Hallelujah. Ephesians 2:16. This is what he did. And I'm going to read it,

> *and that he might reconcile both unto God in one body by the cross, having slain the enmity thereby:*

He slew it, He slew it, He slew the separation, He slew the sin. Jesus slew it! It was slain. Amen. Having slain the enmity thereby. Glory to God! He destroyed it with his blood, with his blood!

Now, my purpose of studying this coming before God was because something was said when one was being delivered, and we were pleading the blood of Jesus. I love to say the blood of Jesus prevails because it does. It bears record. It's witnessing for us right now in the earth and before the throne. God the Father is bearing record in heaven with Jesus Christ and the Holy Spirit. Amen. The word of life. They're bearing record in heaven, but the blood bears record here on earth, and they agree. The word, the water, and the blood, and they agree!

God the Father, Son, and the Holy Spirit are one, and the blood, the word, and the water agree in one. It's at work on our behalf in heaven and in earth. Amen. Now the blood that Jesus shed, remember it's still at work. There's power of resurrection with the blood of Jesus Christ. It's powerful to forgive us of our sins!

It's got to be powerful and not only forgive, but to cleanse us, purifying, purging all the deadness out of us… dead. This is why God says we are lively stones. God's people are alive because the blood hath quickened us. The blood gave us life. Made us aware that we are serving a living God because it has made us alive. The blood of Jesus!

The blood of Jesus. It was the blood that did it! Now remember, Jesus spoke life, Jesus came, he healed the sick, he raised the dead, but they died again. Jesus wrought miracles. Jesus did many fold miracles. He preached, he taught, he did marvelous works that God the Father sent him to do, but not until he died did all that he said and all that he did come into effect, came into force by the power of the blood!

The blood of Jesus wrought it for us. This is why it's so pathetic to hear those who claim they know the Lord, but it's head knowledge. It's head knowledge. The blood hasn't cleansed them, they haven't allowed the blood…Many, many preachers, many are learning in the seminaries today, and they are refuting, they are denying that the blood of Jesus was shed for mankind's sin.

So, they have no life, and yet they say they are learning to preach the gospel. They are learning to be ministers of the gospel of what? Because this is what all Christianity stands upon, the shedding of the blood of Jesus Christ. The blood, without the blood, the shedding of blood, there is no forgiveness, there's no cleansing.

God required a blood sacrifice, and Jesus did it!

He died once. It was accomplished. All that the Mosaic law had tried to do, Jesus finished in six hours… six hours. But it was a lot of work going on… it was a lot of suffering going on… it was a lot of debt being paid. Hallelujah. It was a lot of work being wrought in those six hours that Jesus hung on that tree, dying, shedding his life by drops of blood, drops of blood, drop… drop… drop. Amen. For our sakes, looking at the victory ahead, that's what he did.

That's why he was able to stay on that cross dying. Father, why hast thou forsaken me? But he was looking ahead. He was weakening, weakening. The light was ebbing out of him. Almost gone.

Because the blood was still draining. The blood was still dropping. But Jesus was looking at the victory ahead. Hallelujah!

He was triumphing over sin!

Triumphing over sickness!

Triumphing over disease!

Triumphing over insanity!

Triumphing over lust!

Triumphing over death!

And he spoiled with his blood… Jesus spoiled the principalities and the powers of the devil. Jesus did with his blood, with his blood. Hallelujah.

And let me tell you what the Lord revealed to me. Whenever the devil attacks, whenever he holds a soul in bondage, Jesus is looking for someone to say:

> "The blood of Jesus was shed for this soul's deliverance. The blood prevails against you! The blood of Jesus wars against your hold on this person's life. You've got no right! The blood of Jesus prevails against you!"

And it breaks the hold. Not only the word in Jesus' name. Oh yes, we have to say in Jesus' name, the blood prevails, the blood prevails! Against any diabolical force! Remember when Jesus hung there dying, no matter what he said, the blood was at work, delivering us, saving us, cleansing us, forgiving us. Jesus forgave us long before we asked for forgiveness. Jesus reconciled us long before we came into agreement. Jesus shed his blood, and the blood was saying,

> "They're Gods... They're Gods. I break your power. I break your hold, satan. I break your darkness upon their minds!"

The blood was talking. Remember Abel's blood that talked from the grave, that talked from the ground. Well, if man that is made of the earth, his blood can talk. Why can't the Lord's blood talk? The blood prevails!

The blood was destroying the hold of the devil that he held on the souls and on the minds and on the bodies of mankind, and setting man free. And not until the powers of darkness were spoiled and destroyed, and Jesus triumphing over death. When he said it is finished, he won!

Jesus won over sickness. He won over sin. He won over the world. He won over the powers of darkness. He destroyed the devil and his principalities. Jesus triumphed with the blood!

It is finished! Hallelujah. Hallelujah.

Thank God for the blood. Thank you, Jesus, for the blood. Oh, Lamb of God, thank you for your blood. Thank you for your blood, Lord Jesus. Oh, we love you today. We love you, Jesus.

Thank you, Jesus. Thank you, Jesus.

You see, the blood of the goats and the heifers and so forth, they couldn't destroy the power of sin. They couldn't destroy the hold of the devil. It was only a form, Amen. Or only a pattern to that which Jesus Christ only could come and do. And he did, He accomplished it! Praise God! That's why we are free today!

This is why we can sing We are redeemed. Amen. It was the blood of Jesus, the life that was given for us. Life for our life. Hallelujah. That we would not have to die. Praise God. No Christian dies; we do not die. We just sleep away. Remember what Jesus said of Lazarus? He's asleep. Praise God in the highest. Hallelujah. Hallelujah.

We are not afraid of death. Glory be to God because we know that Jesus has conquered him. Hallelujah. He cannot hold us; Jesus spoiled him openly, made an open, triumphant shame of the devil. Jesus tore him up on that cross! Amen.

Why do you think when he gave up his spirit, when he gave up his ghost, that all the world got dark? Hallelujah.

He brought the principalities and the powers of the air down. They came down! They came tumbling down from the air. Praise God. The life ebbed out of Jesus for our sakes. For all humanity, all humanity. Jesus went down to hell and got the saints that were bound there in Hades in that holding tent of the devil. Where the devil held them captive. Amen. They died in God Jehovah. He couldn't take them to hell, where the flames were. So, he held them by death because death hadn't been conquered.

How do you think, how do you think the witch of Endor was able to summon Samuel? He was in a holding place. Amen. And that old wicked witch, having a familiar spirit, was able to summon the soul of Samuel, amen, from his holding place. But it was all a matter of time that Jesus was going to go down there and say, Come on, I loose you, amen, from death itself. Praise God.

He opened up that holding cells, Hallelujah, and Jesus came and he opened the door and he said, Go home, saints. But before you go, go through Jerusalem. Let them know that I am the resurrection and the life, Hallelujah. Praise the Lord and host. And the saints got up out of their graves…freedom! Liberty! their souls set free, and they went home to glory. But not without testifying, I'm alive! The blood freed me! The blood freed me! Hallelujah, Jesus! Bless your holy name!

So, when we plead the blood in the face of the enemy, what we're doing is tormenting that rascal. We're giving him to know you can't hold them, Hallelujah. The blood prevails against you. All God wants is the consent and the willingness and the yield of that man's mind and soul. Amen. God will take possession of the body. Hallelujah. God will take over. But the one that's bringing deliverance must understand that the blood prevails. The blood prevails!

Don't let anyone make you think that it is erroneous when you say the blood of Jesus against you, devil. Amen. The blood is at work, it's alive, and it's still in force. And as long as there's mankind on the face of this earth, the blood will prevail. It is still in force. Hallelujah.

How do you think the Israelites, the Israelis, are going to be saved after the church is caught up out of here? Amen. There's going to be a great deliverance because they are going to realize that they have been had, that they have been deceived, and that the Messiah has come and the church is gone. And they're going to be waiting for his coming, for his coming to the earth. Amen.

And they're going to look and look at his hands. How did you get these scars? What is the meaning of these scars? And he's going to tell them, I was wounded in the house of my friends. Wounded because they are children of Abraham, and they wounded him. They killed him. But he gave his life.

Prepare me a body, I will redeem man, He did with his blood. And only then, after it was done, were the disciples able to comprehend those glorious teachings. The word of God was in force through the blood…through the blood!

Life came to the mind, life came to the soul, life came to the body, even because all the diseases, amen, all the afflictions and all the infirmities, Jesus bore on his body that we might be made whole. See the blood for what it is!

Ask the Lord's blood to cover your veins where your natural blood flows. Ask the blood of Jesus to intermingle. Glory be to God. The blood prevails! The blood prevails! The blood yet prevails! When the enemy is seeking to afflict you, the blood prevails!

By his stripes, the breaking of his body, the opening of his body. But you know what came out? Blood... blood! The breaking of the Lord's body. When they whipped him, they whipped his back, they whipped him! They tore his body open. The Bible says By his stripes we were healed. We were healed from our trespasses and sins. We were healed from mental illness. We were healed from oppression. We were healed from sickness. We were healed from diseases. We were healed from bondage. Amen!

We are a liberated people. This is why God, when he comes in the midst, he looks for us to be lively stones unto him. None of this stuff. (imitates someone not exhibiting the joy of God)

But instead (waving her hands up high) Live! I'm alive! Amen, Amen. I was looking at, I was looking at my granddaughter today, and she was doing one of these numbers, and she turned around and she did again one of these numbers. And I said, That's the way, Lord, you're showing us how to do it. From little children comes perfect praise. Amen. Hallelujah.

Praise God in the highest. This is why we can rejoice. We can rejoice in him because he's alive and he quickens us. Hallelujah, Amen. All heaven stood back. Jesus said, Know ye not, that I can call unto the Father. And he will send me 12 legions of angels. In other words, to give me a way of escape. But I laid down my life. I lay it down. Amen. No man can take it from me. I lay it down of myself. Amen. If I lay it down, I shall take it up again. And he did. And we are witnesses.

We are witnesses because we are alive. We know it was the blood. We know it was a life that's in the blood. Because we are alive. We can say, yes, Lord. Only you could deliver me from the mess that I was in. Only you could wash that mess out of me. Only you could give me a conscience towards God. Hallelujah. How many times did God reach for us? And we went, no, no, not yet. Amen. Continuing on after the devil and on after death.

Until the Lord got caught hold of us by His Holy Spirit. And said, Turn around! Come to me! And here we come, Lord. I can't do it for myself. It's gotta be you. I come, Lord. I come, Lord. Hallelujah. Hallelujah. Life in the blood. The blood is life. Praise His Holy name. My Lord and my God!

Praise the Lord the host. Thank you, Jesus. My Lord. Should I go further, Lord? Amen. I just want to say this. I think I'll start wrapping it up. So, okay. I looked up the word prevailing or prevail. Prevail means to be the most usual or strongest. To be the stronger, win the victory. That's what prevail means. Prevailing or prevails having superior force or influence. Victories.

And let's look at Hebrews 9 and 17. I got that in the notes. I want to see what's here. Oh, yeah.

> For a testament is of force after men are dead: otherwise it is of no strength at all while the testator liveth.

So, prevailing means having superior force. That's what the blood of Jesus has, a superior force.

> *For a testament is of force after men are dead: otherwise it is of no strength at all while the testator liveth.*

The blood of Jesus prevails today; the blood bears witness to the redemptive work of cavalry. This is what the Lord gave me. Even now, the blood, the blood bears witness to the redemptive work of cavalry…even now.

Let's turn to 1st John 5:8, praise our God, let's read verse 7,

> *For there are three that bear record in heaven, the Father, the Word, and the Holy Ghost: and these three are one. And there are three that bear witness in earth, the Spirit, and the water, and the blood: and these three agree in one. If we receive the witness of men, the witness of God is greater:*

And we know that the blood is the witness, Hallelujah, the witness of God is greater… Now look at Revelations 12. I'll show you, show you something. Revelations 12, verse 11. Let's look at verse 10 to get a clearer understanding of verse 11. He says,

> *And I heard a loud voice saying in heaven, Now is come salvation, and strength, and the kingdom of our God, and the power of his Christ: for the accuser of our brethren is cast down, which accused them before our God day and night. And they overcame him by the blood of the Lamb*

You see this? Amen. If you want deliverance, remember the blood of Jesus. If you want triumphant victory, remember the force that's in the blood of Jesus. That's how we overcome the devil. Amen. I don't care whether he's outside or inside. You hear me? We know it's the power of God, the power of Jesus' name, the power of his blood, the power of his word that will bring deliverance.

But don't underestimate the power of the blood because without the blood, nothing else was in operation in the fullness. Nothing was in the fullness. Nothing was complete without the operation of the shedding of the blood of Jesus Christ.

> *And they overcame him by the blood of the Lamb and by the word of their testimony.*

What do they testify to? What do they testify to? What does the witness of Jesus Christ testify to? That there is power in the blood, that the blood of Jesus was shed. Amen. And that's what we hold against the accuser. He thinks he's got a hold on the souls that God has made. Not if that soul wants deliverance. Amen.

And we testify that the blood of Jesus is in force against him. Amen. The blood prevails! The blood prevails. Let me read this again. Prevail, to be the most usual or strongest, to be the stronger, win the victory. Prevailing, having superior force or influence, victories.

> *For a testament,*

Hebrews 9:17,

> *For a testament is of force after men are dead. Otherwise, it is of no strength at all while the testator liveth.*

The blood of Jesus prevails today. The blood bears witness to the redemptive work of Calvary. And there are three that bear witness in earth, the spirit and the water and the blood. And these three agree in one. And revelations again, 12 verse 11.

> *And they overcame him by the blood of the Lamb, and by the word of their testimony; and they loved not their lives unto the death.*

You know why? Because a real child of God is not afraid of death. How do you think those saints... Jesus had said before he left this earth, how many would be martyred, how they would be killed, amen. How they would have to give their lives, and even how they would have to run from city to city until it was time for them to leave this earth. Because men would hate them.

They had the mind of the devil. And we see men with the mind of the devil today. There is nothing right but Jesus Christ in this earth, Amen. The minds are under darkness. I don't care how intelligent they say they are. If they are not under the Lord Jesus Christ, they are of darkness. And we see what darkness, we see what darkened minds have done to this earth. They themselves witnessed that this earth is in turmoil. That this earth is a mess. And the earth itself is groaning for redemption, Amen. The earth itself is hurting, praise God. Look at the trees, look at the things that God has created on this earth. They're groaning because of sin, because of the darkness of mankind.

Because of the destruction that man and man alone is bringing. The animals didn't bring the destruction. Mankind, under the powers of darkness, gross darkness have brought this earth to its present condition. And Jesus will come to set it in order. But we that are here, we're redeemed by the blood. We carry the blood in our bodies.

Amen. Not only is our name written with blood in the Lamb's Book of Life. But we carry the blood of Jesus in us and upon us. We are cleansed every day with the blood and the water and the word. Hallelujah.

They are bearing record right now on our behalf by the Holy Ghost. The Holy Ghost is putting all of this that Jesus has accomplished into effect on our behalf. Amen.

That's why we should cherish the Holy Ghost. We should cherish him. He's not only given for us to speak in new tongues. Amen. That's only the beginning. Praise God! But I tell you the work of the Holy Spirit is most valuable to the living Christ in us today. And on our behalf. Valuable! Valuable! Because Jesus sent him. God the Father, God the Son sent the Holy Spirit to reinforce that which was already put in force. Amen. And he's doing a good job. He's doing a marvelous job.

Hallelujah. Thank God for the Holy Ghost. Thank God for the Holy Ghost. And he understanding that Jesus and Jesus Christ alone accomplished that work of redemption. He will not speak for himself. He speaks of Jesus! What Jesus has done. He reveals Jesus to us because of the blood. And we can thank God for Jesus!

God so loved us that he gave that sacrifice. He sent Jesus to be that sacrifice. He was without Jesus, being right near him in heaven, working with him for 33 and some years. But oh, what a rejoicing. What a jubilee! When Jesus entered back into heaven. To his rightful place of deity! With God the Father. Amen. But Jesus brought us in his heart. He just didn't come down and sit down beside the Father in his glory and say the Holy Ghost is sitting now.

And he's doing the work. But Jesus remembers what he suffered there on that cross for us.

Jesus is that great high priest, amen, pleading our causes before the God that made us. Jesus, this tender loving king of glory. This merciful great high priest is pleading for you and me. He's our mediator, Hallelujah. He is our redemption right now, pleading for us to have the victory. To know the victory, to enter in triumphantly. To walk in this earth as kings and priests, redeemed by his blood. Praise our God in the highest. Oh, Lamb of God, I praise you today!

I praise you, Jesus. I magnify your name. Bless your sweet name, Lord Jesus. Oh, Lamb of God, thank you for who you are. Thank you for the blood today. Thank you, Jesus. My soul magnifies you, Lord. Hallelujah. Hallelujah. Oh, Lamb of God, I thank you for your blood. Let your blood be applied. Let your blood be applied. Bless your holy name, Lord. Oh, sweet Jesus. Sweet Jesus.

Sweet Jesus. Oh, adorable king of glory. Hallelujah. Oh, your precious blood. Thank you for shedding your precious blood. Thank you, Jesus. Thank you for the life that you gave that we might live. Oh, son of the living God. The pillar in the ground of truth. Thank you for the atonement. Thank you for being there, Oh, in the throne room of God. Sitting on his mighty throne. Making intercessions for us. Thank you that we can come in your name, knowing the redemptive work of Calvary is for our sakes. Thank you, Jesus.

You said that when you see the blood, you would pass over the Israelites. Oh, let your blood be applied. When your judgments are in the earth, Lord. Let your blood be applied continually upon us and over us, in us… Oh, that we might be spared from these calamities that are yet to come.

Thank you. Thank you, Jesus. Praises unto you, My Lord and my God. Hallelujah. Oh, the blood of Jesus, it washes white as snow. Glory to God. Let the blood of Jesus wash you, sinner. Let the blood prevail on your behalf today. Let the blood of Jesus wash you, sinner. Let the blood of Jesus comfort you. Let the blood prevail against every stain, against every spot. Against every blemish.

God loves you! He wants to cleanse you. Hallelujah. The blood, that's power of deliverance. Hallelujah. You've been redeemed already; put it into effect in your personal life. Let the blood of Jesus cover you right now. Give yourself to him. Hallelujah. Oh, He'll wash you today. He'll forgive you today. Hallelujah. The blood will wash from all stains and guile, no matter how deep the stain. The blood will prevail. The blood will cleanse.

The blood will make you whole today. Hallelujah Jesus. If you want life, receive Jesus Christ. Amen. Receive him!

Believe on the Lord thy God. Believe what he's done for you in Calvary. The blood prevails, Hallelujah. It is still in force today. Glory to God! It's still in force! It still is in force for you. Hallelujah.

Let His will be done. Hallelujah. Let him in!

Let him do his work in you. Glory to God. That's right. Let him in… Let him in!

Let the Lord Jesus in.

Jesus Came to Lift Up On High

First Aired Oct 23, 1996

God the Father sent Jesus into this world that we might have life. So I want to minister today concerning the purpose of the coming of the Messiah. My title will be Jesus came to lift us up on high. This is his sole purpose in coming to this earth, amen. Isaiah chapter 7 verse 14 tells us,

> *Therefore the Lord himself shall give you a sign;*
> *Behold, a virgin shall conceive, and bear a son, and*
> *shall call his name Immanuel. Butter and honey*
> *shall he eat, that he may know to refuse the evil, and*
> *choose the good.*

That he may know to refuse all the evil of this world and choose that which is good and acceptable in the eyes of the most high God, amen. We know also in Isaiah chapter 9, the word of God says in verse 6,

> *For unto us a child is born, unto us a son is given:*
> *and the government shall be upon his shoulder: and*
> *his name shall be called Wonderful, Counsellor, The*
> *mighty God, The everlasting Father, The Prince of*
> *Peace. Of the increase of his government and*
> *peace there shall be no end, upon the throne of*
> *David, and upon his kingdom, to order it, and to*
> *establish it with judgment and with justice from*
> *henceforth even for ever. The zeal of the LORD of*
> *hosts will perform this.*

The zeal of the Lord of hosts will perform this. Isaiah the prophet of God, prophesying of Christ Jesus, Christ Immanuel, Jesus, Immanuel God with us, Christ the anointed one, Jesus the Savior of all mankind. Isaiah chapter 11 tells us,

And there shall come forth a rod out of the stem of Jesse, and a branch shall grow out of his roots.

> *And there shall come forth a rod out of the stem of Jesse, and a Branch shall grow out of his roots: and the Spirit of the LORD shall rest upon him, the spirit of wisdom and understanding, the spirit of counsel and might, the spirit of knowledge and of the fear of the LORD; and shall make him of quick understanding in the fear of the LORD: and he shall not judge after the sight of his eyes, neither reprove after the hearing of his ears: but with righteousness shall he judge the poor, and reprove with equity for the meek of the earth: and he shall smite the earth with the rod of his mouth, and with the breath of his lips shall he slay the wicked. And righteousness shall be the girdle of his loins, and faithfulness the girdle of his reins.*

This is the Christ, the Messiah, our Savior, who is called Jesus. Amen. Over in St. Luke, in the New Testament chapter 1, the Word of God tells us in verse 28,

> *And the angel came in unto her, and said, Hail, thou that art highly favoured, the Lord is with thee: blessed art thou among women. And when she saw him, she was troubled at his saying, and cast in her mind what manner of salutation this should be. And the angel said unto her, Fear not, Mary: for*

thou hast found favour with God. And, behold, thou shalt conceive in thy womb, and bring forth a son, and shalt call his name JESUS. He shall be great, and shall be called the Son of the Highest: and the Lord God shall give unto him the throne of his father David: and he shall reign over the house of Jacob for ever; and of his kingdom there shall be no end.

We read that in the book of Isaiah.

Then said Mary unto the angel, How shall this be, seeing I know not a man? And the angel answered and said unto her, The Holy Ghost shall come upon thee, and the power of the Highest shall overshadow thee: therefore also that holy thing which shall be born of thee shall be called the Son of God. And, behold, thy cousin Elisabeth, she hath also conceived a son in her old age: and this is the sixth month with her, who was called barren. For with God nothing shall be impossible.

FOR WITH GOD NOTHING IS IMPOSSIBLE!,

And Mary said, Behold the handmaid of the Lord; be it unto me according to thy word. And the angel departed from her.

And Mary arose in those days, and went into the hill country with haste, into a city of Juda; and entered into the house of Zacharias, and saluted Elisabeth. And it came to pass, that, when Elisabeth heard the salutation of Mary, the babe leaped in her womb; and Elisabeth was filled with the Holy Ghost: and she spake out with a loud voice, and said, Blessed art thou among women, and blessed is the fruit of thy womb. And whence is this to me, that the mother of my Lord should come to me? For, lo, as soon as the voice of thy salutation sounded in mine ears, the babe leaped in my womb for joy. And blessed is she that believed: for there shall be a performance of those things which were told her from the Lord.

And Mary said, My soul doth magnify the Lord, And my spirit hath rejoiced in God my Saviour. For he hath regarded the low estate of his handmaiden: For, behold, from henceforth all generations shall call me blessed. For he that is mighty hath done to me great things; And holy is his name. And his mercy is on them that fear him. From generation to generation.

He hath shewed strength with his arm; He hath scattered the proud in the imagination of their hearts. He hath put down the mighty from their seats, And exalted them of low degree. He hath filled the hungry with good things; And the rich he hath sent empty away.

He hath holpen his servant Israel, In remembrance of his mercy; As he spake to our fathers, To Abraham, and to his seed for ever. And Mary abode with her about three months, and returned to her own house.

Amen. And then after Elizabeth, Mary's cousin, had given birth to John, the prophet of the Most High God, the Lord opened Elizabeth's husband's mouth, and he was able to speak. In verse 67,

*And his father Zacharias was filled with the Holy
Ghost, and prophesied, saying, Blessed be the Lord
God of Israel; For he hath visited and redeemed his
people, And hath raised up an horn of salvation for
us. In the house of his servant David; As he spake
by the mouth of his holy prophets, which have been
since the world began: That we should be saved
from our enemies, and from the hand of all that hate
us; To perform the mercy promised to our fathers,
And to remember his holy covenant; The oath which
he sware to our father Abraham, That he would
grant unto us, that we being delivered out of the
hand of our enemies Might serve him without fear,
In holiness and righteousness before him, all the
days of our life.*

And speaking to his baby John, he says,

*And thou, child, shalt be called the prophet of the
Highest: For thou shalt go before the face of the
Lord to prepare his ways; To give knowledge of
salvation unto his people By the remission of their
sins,*

This was John's task, to prepare the way of the Lord, as the
book of Malachi, the prophet Malachi, foretold.

*Through the tender mercy of our God; Whereby the
dayspring from on high hath visited us,*

Amen. The dayspring from on high, John of earthly
parents, came forth from godly and righteous parents. But
Jesus Christ is called the dayspring from on high. For the
Holy Ghost overshadowed Mary and not man.

31

the dayspring from on high hath visited us, To give light to them that sit in darkness and in the shadow of death, To guide our feet into the way of peace.

Jesus came to lift us up on high.

And the child grew, and waxed strong in spirit, and was in the deserts till the day of his shewing unto Israel.

Praise our God. And we hear of the birth of Jesus Christ in verse 6, chapter 2 of Luke.

And so it was, that, while they were there, the days were accomplished that she should be delivered.

They had traveled into Bethlehem to pay taxes. And verse 7,

And she brought forth her firstborn son, and wrapped him in swaddling clothes, and laid him in a manger; because there was no room for them in the inn.

And there were in the same country shepherds abiding in the field, keeping watch over their flock by night. And, lo, the angel of the Lord came upon them, and the glory of the Lord shone round about them: and they were sore afraid. And the angel said unto them, Fear not: for, behold, I bring you good tidings of great joy, which shall be to all people.

To all people, and that's the gospel today. Jesus is that joy to all people. All nations, all nationalities, all races, all kinds of people throughout all the earth.

To all people.

> *For unto you is born this day in the city of David a Saviour, which is Christ the Lord. And this shall be a sign unto you; Ye shall find the babe wrapped in swaddling clothes, lying in a manger. And suddenly there was with the angel a multitude of the heavenly host praising God, and saying,*
>
> *Glory to God in the highest, And on earth peace, good will toward men.*

The angels, the heavenly host of God, singing the glorious praises because of the birth of Jesus and the purpose of His coming. Peace and goodwill toward men. That was the Father's purpose in sending Christ Jesus: to grant mankind peace. And peace can only come as we receive God's love gift. Jesus Christ, the anointed one, the day spring from on high. The word of God says,

> *And it came to pass, as the angels were gone away from them into heaven, the shepherds said one to another, Let us now go even unto Bethlehem, and see this thing which is come to pass, which the Lord hath made known unto us.*

And that's one thing about God. He has a way of getting His word across to mankind, amen. God has a people that will believe the gospel. Hallelujah. God has a people that will believe in miracles. It was a miracle that Mary, the virgin, conceived Christ by the Holy Ghost and brought Him into this world by the Holy Ghost. It's a miracle.

But we believe in miracles, don't we? Because we believe that Jesus came as the Savior of the world. Amen. We saw the miracle of salvation in our hearts and in our souls, in our minds, freeing us from the cares of this life, didn't we? Amen. There is a people that will believe their God. Hallelujah. And we thank God for the report that is given concerning Christ Jesus.

Amen and amen. Now Simeon, over in verse 25,

> *And, behold, there was a man in Jerusalem, whose name was Simeon; and the same man was just and devout, waiting for the consolation of Israel: and the Holy Ghost was upon him. And it was revealed unto him by the Holy Ghost, that he should not see death, before he had seen the Lord's Christ. And he came by the Spirit into the temple: and when the parents brought in the child Jesus, to do for him after the custom of the law, then took he him up in his arms, and blessed God, and said,*
>
> *Lord, now lettest thou thy servant depart in peace, According to thy word: For mine eyes have seen thy salvation,*

Here is a devout priest of God named Simeon waiting because the Holy Ghost had promised him that he would not see death until he had seen the Lord's Christ, the salvation of Israel, and the salvation of the world.

> *For mine eyes have seen thy salvation, Which thou hast prepared before the face of all people; A light to lighten the Gentiles, And the glory of thy people Israel.*

Jesus is that light that came into this darkened world. And Jesus is yet shining brightly, amen, in this world to those that love him. And he has illuminated us, amen, that have accepted him and received, amen, the Lord Jesus Christ, the anointed one from on high. Glory be to God. Jesus came to cause our eyes to see. He came to cause our ears to hear.

He came to cause our hearts to hope, to bring peace where there is enmity, to exalt the lowly, amen, to bring us goodwill, to give us knowledge of the holy. This is why Jesus came. Praise his holy name, amen. Therefore, the Lord himself shall give you a sign, the word of God says, and we know that that sign was given because the Holy Ghost has witnessed that truth in our hearts. Man would say, Prove it, and I'll believe it. The Holy Ghost said, Believe it, and I'll prove it.

Glory to God, and we believe. And it's proven in our hearts. Call us whatever you will, but we know that Jesus has come. We know he is that Messiah. We know he is that prophet of God. We know he is that mighty deliverer. We know he is our soon coming king. We know he is the Lord of lords. We know he is the king of kings. We know that he is the maker and the creator with the almighty Father. Glory be to God, we know, amen, that Jesus is coming to receive us unto himself. Praise the Lord of hosts, amen.

He came to be our savior, amen. And the word of God says in Matthew 1:21,

> *And she shall bring forth a son, and thou shalt call his name JESUS: for he shall save his people from their sins.*

Jesus came to raise us from the natural way, amen, of living, to his spiritual way of living. Jesus came to awaken us and reveal unto us the Father's glorious kingdom. Jesus came to raise our expectations, amen, and give us the true meaning of life. He is the Lord of faith, for he is the author and the finisher of our faith.

He came to make us the head and not the tail. He came to make us joint heirs with him. We're heirs with the children of God, and we're heirs of the most high God, and we're joint heirs with Jesus Christ, amen, with Christ... with Christ! Jesus came to lift us up on high. Glory to God. We're not weakly, beggarly people of this earth. Jesus has made us to be kings and priests in his Father's kingdom. We have hope! We have life everlasting!

We have joy unspeakable and full of glory. This is why Jesus came, to bring us out of the natural, the natural way of thinking. This world is bombarded with the cares of this life. Glory be to God. They're out there begging for a drop of water, amen, and a morsel of bread. Praise God, but Jesus came that we might have life, and that more abundantly, amen.

He left his riches in glory to make us rich on the face of this earth, rich in the things of the most high God. We have inherited the kingdom of God through Jesus Christ our Lord, amen. This is why Jesus came, to bring us from the earthly, amen, to the heavenly.

Glory be to God. We all should rejoice, and we should go and tell everybody, everywhere that Jesus has come, amen. And we don't stop there. We tell them Jesus is coming again to receive us unto himself, amen. He's coming on that cloud, amen, with the glory that he had with the Father before the world began. Glory, hallelujah.

Jesus is coming, amen and amen. Blessed be his holy name. Oh, glory to God. For this cause, Jesus came to lift us up on high. Amen, to give us that great expectation that we don't have to live with bowed down heads. Glory be to God, and a wayward heart.

Jesus came to make our path straight. He came to be that light unto us, and he's shining unto us. Jesus shines evermore. Glory to his name. We don't have to grow up in darkness anymore. Glory, hallelujah. We do not have to ponder, amen, which way we should take. But Jesus said he is the way, the truth, and the life. Glory, hallelujah. And it's one thing about Jesus, he is the truth indeed. Praise God, he cannot speak a lie because truth fills him through and through. Praise God, and we shall know him, amen.

If we should follow on to seek him, we shall know in whom we believe. Just as Jesus waxed strong and grew in favor with God and with man, he waxed strong and bold in the wisdom of the most high God and in knowledge and understanding. And we are like Jesus in this earth. As Jesus was the express image of God his father, amen, so are we being joint heirs with him. We are the express image of the most high God, Jesus Christ, our everlasting king.

He's coming for us. Bless his holy name, amen, to usher us into the Father's glorious kingdom. For this cause, Jesus came to lift us up on high. Let's go. Let's go back with him. Let's take courage, amen. Let's believe God. Let's take hold of faith, amen, and go back with him, for he's coming to lift us up on high.

TRUE BREAD

First Aired on May 8th, 2006

Greetings, everyone. We praise God for this opportunity to come in your way again. And we thank the Lord for His goodness and His mercies that He has abundantly bestowed upon us.

He is a good God. Always, I shall proclaim that God is a good God. I am your evangelist, Martha P. Davis, thanking God for this opportunity to bring the word of life unto His people once more and again.

We thank the Lord for all of you who are listening to God's holy mountain broadcast. We thank God for your precious support, prayers, and supplications on our behalf. It is most welcome, and we truly thank you over and over again.

Even in our prayers, we thank God for you. Turn with me to the sixth chapter of John, the Gospel of John, glory to God.

In the name of Jesus, Father, we come before the throne of grace, thanking you for this opportunity. Amen, and we give you the glory and the honor and the praise that's due unto you. Hallelujah. Have your mighty way and send forth your anointing upon us all. As we minister your word today and as we receive, Lord, give us ears to hear. And give us a heart to accept that, that you have to say.

Have preeminence over every one of us, we're yours, Lord. And some may be listening who have not known you as their personal saviors yet. Lord, I ask by your spirit that you draw them. Glory, hallelujah. Draw them unto you, and let them hear the word of the Lord and be set free. Give them a home in your kingdom, we pray. In the glorious name of Jesus, amen and amen. The word of God says, John chapter six,

After these things Jesus went over the sea of Galilee, which is the sea of Tiberias. 2And a great multitude followed him, because they saw his miracles which he did on them that were diseased. And Jesus went up into a mountain, and there he sat with his disciples. And the passover, a feast of the Jews, was nigh.

When Jesus then lifted up his eyes, and saw a great company come unto him, he saith unto Philip, Whence shall we buy bread, that these may eat? And this he said to prove him: for he himself knew what he would do. Philip answered him, Two

hundred pennyworth of bread is not sufficient for them, that every one of them may take a little.

One of his disciples, Andrew, Simon Peter's brother, saith unto him, There is a lad here, which hath five barley loaves, and two small fishes: but what are they among so many? And Jesus said, Make the men sit down. Now there was much grass in the place. So the men sat down, in number about five thousand.

And Jesus took the loaves; and when he had given thanks, he distributed to the disciples, and the disciples to them that were set down; and likewise of the fishes as much as they would. When they were filled, he said unto his disciples, Gather up the fragments that remain, that nothing be lost. Therefore they gathered them together, and filled twelve baskets with the fragments of the five barley loaves, which remained over and above unto them that had eaten. Then those men, when they had seen the miracle that Jesus did, said, This is of a truth that prophet that should come into the world.

When Jesus therefore perceived that they would come and take him by force, to make him a king, he departed again into a mountain himself alone. And when even was now come, his disciples went down unto the sea, and entered into a ship, and went over the sea toward Capernaum. And it was now dark, and Jesus was not come to them. And the sea arose by reason of a great wind that blew. So when they had rowed about five and twenty or thirty furlongs, they see Jesus walking on the sea, and drawing nigh unto the ship: and they were afraid. But he saith unto them, It is I; be not afraid. Then they willingly received him into the ship: and immediately the ship was at the land whither they went.

The day following, when the people which stood on the other side of the sea saw that there was none other boat there, save that one whereinto his disciples were entered, and that Jesus went not with his disciples into the boat, but that his disciples were gone away alone; (howbeit there came other boats from Tiberias nigh unto the place where they did eat bread, after that the Lord had given thanks:) when the people therefore saw that Jesus was not there, neither his disciples, they also took shipping, and came to Capernaum, seeking for Jesus.

And when they had found him on the other side of the sea, they said unto him, Rabbi, when camest thou hither? Jesus answered them and said, Verily, verily, I say unto you, Ye seek me, not because ye saw the miracles, but because ye did eat of the loaves, and were filled. Labour not for the meat which perisheth, but for that meat which endureth unto everlasting life, which the Son of man shall give unto you: for him hath God the Father sealed.

Then said they unto him, What shall we do, that we might work the works of God? Jesus answered and said unto them, This is the work of God, that ye believe on him whom he hath sent.

Meaning God the Father. Now, what the Lord is saying to them as he is saying to us today through the written word. This is why I take time to read the word that you may get a clear picture of what God is saying to us today, because it's written down that we too may see and read, and understand.

Many, many people are following God for what they can get on this side of the kingdom, meaning here on earth. They want the blessings of God. They want the natural blessings. And there's nothing wrong with that, if it's put in the right perspective, we need to live on this earth.

And God has promised to meet our every need, according to his riches in glory, as we ask of him. We must ask in prayer, believing. But that's not the real reason the Lord wants us to see the deeper meaning of this word. What Jesus says, Labor not for the meat which perisheth, but for that meat which endureth unto everlasting life. You see, Jesus is our everlasting life. He is that bread from heaven. He is our redeemer.

And after we depart from this natural life, living here on this earth, even though we're heaven-bound, we've been born again by his spirit. Glory be to God. He is telling us to do better than this. Look for greater things, look to please God that we may enter into his kingdom when he comes for us.

For Jesus is coming. And his coming is very near. And the Lord just kept putting this scripture on my heart to bring forth to you today. Labor not for the meat that perishes, for that is not going to get us into the kingdom. But labor, be pleasing to God. Labor to win God. How do we win him? By obeying his will. Seeing the spiritual things, the things that are everlasting, even now. He doesn't want our vision to be short-sighted.

He wants us to look beyond the now and see what he's done for us. When he went to that cross, glory be to God, and shed his blood and gave up his life that we might live, that we might live. And we'll read on further. You may get a greater understanding. They asked him, I'll read again.

> *This is the work of God, that ye believe on him whom he hath sent.*

That's Jesus answering them when they wanted to know, What shall we do that we might work the works of God? Hallelujah. See, Jesus, Jesus is sure and he's sound, He doesn't tell us things or do things for us, you know, to just please us and tickle our ears. That's not the purpose of his coming. The purpose of his coming is that we might please God, that we might have the power to please God, that we might have the discipline by the Holy Spirit to please God. Only those that God takes pleasure in, that pleases him, that obeys him, will enter into the kingdom of God in heaven.

When Jesus comes in the air on that glorious cloud to receive those that are waiting and watching for him and that have labored up to that very moment in faith, believing. He wants our eyes off the things of this earth. Glory, hallelujah.

And let our goal be set in our hearts and in our minds that we are here to please God. We laid down our lives. Amen. We lay ourselves before God, and he guides us daily. We seek to please him every day of our lives by believing on him. Everything that he has done, believe it. Jesus said, You're not following me for the miracles. Jesus Christ worked miracles. He said, but for the fishes and the loaves.

That was a bad choice. And many are making bad choices today. And the Lord is saying, Hear what I'm saying to you. Don't follow me for what you can get now. But obey me, believe who I am, who I say I am, believe on me and the works that I do, you shall do also. Be about your father's business. I came to bring you life and to work the works of God, to perform the miracles that God has performed, God the Son, as God the Father sent him into this earth. He said to his disciples, Greater works than these shall you do because I go to my father. What greater works? Continuing the work of the kingdom of God in heaven.

We continue it on this earth, bringing deliverance to the captives. Glory, hallelujah. And to preach Jesus Christ, the only Savior of all mankind. He is the only savior. And Jesus said, This is the work of God that you believe on him whom he hath sent, the Father hath sent.

> *They said therefore unto him, What sign shewest thou then, that we may see, and believe thee? what dost thou work? Our fathers did eat manna in the desert; as it is written, He gave them bread from heaven to eat. Then Jesus said unto them, Verily, verily, I say unto you, Moses gave you not that bread from heaven; but my Father giveth you the true bread from heaven. For the bread of God is he which cometh down from heaven, and giveth life unto the world.*

The bread of God, the bread from God's throne, is Jesus Christ.

> *Then said they unto him, Lord, evermore give us this bread. 35And Jesus said unto them, I am the bread of life:*

I am the bread of life.

> *he that cometh to me shall never hunger; and he*
> *that believeth on me shall never thirst.*

Never.

> *But I said unto you, That ye also have seen me, and*
> *believe not.*

See how God knows the heart? Many are receiving from
him even today, and they still do not believe on him. The
breath we breathe is God's. The strength that we have to go
about our personal affairs is God's. And many will not give
him the honor because they do not even believe he exists.
We look at all of this nonsense that's going on concerning
the Da Vinci Code. Just lies from the pit of hell because
satan knows that his time is short and he's coming out with
all kinds of diabolical lies because of man's unbelief. It's
easy for satan to win because man's heart is full of unbelief.
Hallelujah.

But Jesus is that true bread. He is our bread from heaven.
And all that Jesus spoke, he was ordained by the Father to
come and say unto us, there's a reckoning day coming. And
Jesus has come to give us life before that reckoning day
soon comes. Hallelujah. He said, Jesus said unto them,

I am the bread of life.

I repeat. Hallelujah.

> *he that cometh to me shall never hunger; and he*
> *that believeth on me shall never thirst. But I said*
> *unto you, That ye also have seen me, and believe*
> *not. All that the Father giveth me shall come to me;*
> *and him that cometh to me I will in no wise cast out.*

 Just come. Come unto him. Believe on him as the gospel
has said. As I'm reading today.

> *For I came down from heaven, not to do mine own*
> *will, but the will of him that sent me. And this is the*
> *Father's will which hath sent me, that of all which*
> *he hath given me I should lose nothing, but should*
> *raise it up again at the last day. And this is the will*
> *of him that sent me, that every one which seeth the*
> *Son,*

That means to see with the spiritual eye, perceive in the
heart who Jesus is.

that every one which seeth the Son, and believeth on
him, may have everlasting life: and I will raise him
up at the last day.

That's a promise to everyone who has received him
according to the gospel of Jesus Christ. Not what some
other one is saying. But Jesus, the true bread, he is our life
indeed. Because if we tried to live without eating in the
natural, we would die of famine. If we would try to live
without drinking, we would die of thirst.

But Jesus is offering us, everyone across the world, around
the world, everlasting life. The price is already paid. And
all we have to do is believe the gospel. If you don't believe
who's portraying the word of God, who's bringing the word
of God, who's preaching or teaching the word of God, get
the Bible and read for yourself and believe the word of
God. It's so important. It's so important.

Because what you believe will determine where you will
spend eternity. Believe on the Lord Jesus Christ and receive
him. He said,

> *The Jews then murmured at him, because he said, I*
> *am the bread which came down from heaven. And*

they said, Is not this Jesus, the son of Joseph, whose
father and mother we know? how is it then that he
saith, I came down from heaven?

See, man in his feeble mind, thinking he's so wise, think he knows the answer. They did not know what God had done because they refused to believe.

Jesus therefore answered and said unto
them, Murmur not among yourselves. No man can
come to me, except the Father which hath sent me
draw him: and I will raise him up at the last day. It
is written in the prophets, And they shall be all
taught of God. Every man therefore that hath heard,
and hath learned of the Father, cometh unto me.

If we have truly learned, we will come to the Savior of the world.

Not that any man hath seen the Father, save he
which is of God, he hath seen the Father.

speaking of himself.

Verily, verily, I say unto you, He that believeth on me hath everlasting life. I am that bread of life. Your fathers did eat manna in the wilderness, and are dead. This is the bread which cometh down from heaven, that a man may eat thereof, and not die.

meaning himself.

I am the living bread which came down from heaven: if any man eat of this bread, he shall live for ever: and the bread that I will give is my flesh, which I will give for the life of the world.

And he did, on that old rugged cross, when he could have called for twelve legions of angels. But he chose to obey the father, because God so loved the world... His love is great towards mankind, and he sent his best. He sent his only begotten son. Hallelujah. To die for us, that we might live. To shed his blood, that we might have life everlasting. And all we have to do is believe on him. Believe his word.

I am the living bread,

I repeat,

*which came down from heaven: if any man eat of
this bread, he shall live for ever: and the bread that
I will give is my flesh, which I will give for the life
of the world.*

*The Jews therefore strove among themselves,
saying, How can this man give us his flesh to
eat? Then Jesus said unto them, Verily, verily, I say
unto you, Except ye eat the flesh of the Son of man,
and drink his blood, ye have no life in you. Whoso
eateth my flesh, and drinketh my blood, hath eternal
life; and I will raise him up at the last day.*

He repeats it again.

*For my flesh is meat indeed, and my blood is drink
indeed.*

See, it's all by faith, precious ones, believing his word.
And he does a marvelous work of salvation in us because
we believe on him. When we come and surrender our lives,
knowing that he is the Savior that God the Father has sent
unto the children of men worldwide. We eat of him and we

drink of him, spiritually, spiritually. My flesh is meat indeed, and my blood is drink indeed. He said in verse 56,

> *He that eateth my flesh, and drinketh my blood, dwelleth in me, and I in him. As the living Father hath sent me, and I live by the Father: so he that eateth me, even he shall live by me.*

No other…

> *This is that bread which came down from heaven: not as your fathers did eat manna, and are dead: he that eateth of this bread shall live for ever. These things said he in the synagogue, as he taught in Capernaum.*
> *Many therefore of his disciples, when they had heard this, said, This is an hard saying; who can hear it?*

> *When Jesus knew in himself that his disciples murmured at it, he said unto them, Doth this offend you? What and if ye shall see the Son of man ascend up where he was before? It is the spirit that quickeneth; the flesh profiteth nothing:*

And please understand this, the flesh and all we do in our mortal being profited nothing if we do not know who Jesus is and have received him as our life, our life indeed.

> *It is the spirit that quickeneth; the flesh profiteth nothing: the words that I speak unto you, they are spirit, and they are life.*

We only live by the words that Jesus has come to speak unto us.

> *But there are some of you that believe not. For Jesus knew from the beginning who they were that believed not, and who should betray him. And he said, Therefore said I unto you, that no man can come unto me, except it were given unto him of my Father.*

Hallelujah.

> *no man can come unto me, except it were given unto him of my Father.*
>
> *From that time many of his disciples went back, and walked no more with him. Then said Jesus unto the twelve, Will ye also go away? Then Simon Peter*

answered him, Lord, to whom shall we go? thou
hast the words of eternal life.

Hallelujah.

thou hast the words of eternal life. And we believe
and are sure that thou art that Christ, the Son of the
living God. Jesus answered them, Have not I chosen
you twelve, and one of you is a devil? He spake of
Judas Iscariot the son of Simon: for he it was that
should betray him, being one of the twelve.

Oh, precious ones, believe in the Lord Jesus Christ with all
your heart. Time is winding up. The day of the rapture is
soon approaching us. We call it the rapture. But it's being
caught up to meet him according to Thessalonians. The
book of Thessalonians. Get ready, stay ready. Obey God.
The coming of the Lord is near. Eat the true bread, and
drink the precious blood, and live. Live eternal. Eternally
with the most high God and his Christ. God be with you as
you seek his face. In Jesus' mighty name. Amen. And
amen.

ARISE, SHINE THE GLORY OF THE LORD IS RISEN

First Aired February 5ᵗʰ, 1989

Praise God, thank you Lord, everyone pray. Father, in the name of Jesus, enlighten our hearts that we might receive your word. Let your light shine brightly in us and help us, Lord, to understand the scriptures, in Jesus' name. Isaiah 60:1,

> *Arise, shine; for thy light is come, and the glory of the LORD is risen upon thee.*

So you see, it's not just the song, it's the word, it's the word. Now, when the Lord tells us to arise, that means get up with healing in our innermost being. Get up with strength, get up with power, and shine, shine for his glory, shine for the glory of the Lord is upon us. We are glad because he is shining upon us. You see, we are in his glory, and that glorifies him in heaven and in earth. The angels are looking upon the children of God on the earth, and they are marveling that God Almighty, God the Son, God the Savior of this world, is shining his glory from heaven upon us. Everybody cannot be partaker of this glory, only those that have known Jesus in the pardon of their sins, you see, those that are going wholeheartedly after him. Praise God, the glory of the Lord is risen, and God is saying from on high by his spirit through the prophet Isaiah, Arise, amen. That's why no one should be sitting, singing that song, amen.

If you're singing with understanding, see, we're not just in here being morbid, we are alive, and what we do, we do with all of our heart, and we do with understanding. The Bible tells us in all our getting, get what… understanding, amen. So when we sing in the spirit, we sing with understanding, praise God.

If you don't know what you're singing, you don't listen to it carefully and prayerfully and say, Lord, what is that? What's the meaning of that song? Then ask the Holy Spirit to quicken you to understand, and bless God, you'll understand. Thank God, and in that word that you're singing will become alive to you and become personal to you. Many songs we identify with because of the trials that we go through or heartaches or whatever, but we don't want to just identify with God because of tribulation, we want to rejoice in the Lord our God, we want to be glad for Him, amen, at all times.

That's the secret of your inner strength, praise God, is to be glad for Jesus, did you know that? Amen. If you are glad for Him, honey, you can go through anything. You can take anything, you can do it because you are glad for Jesus, and when you are glad for Him, God is glad that you are glad for Him, amen, and bless God, He will empower you with more joy to be glad, amen! For He says, verse two,

> *For, behold, the darkness shall cover the earth, and gross darkness the people: but the LORD shall arise upon thee, and his glory shall be seen upon thee.*

Now isn't that marvelous? Let's go through that verse again,

> *For, behold, the darkness shall cover the earth, and gross darkness the people: but the LORD shall arise upon thee, and his glory shall be seen upon thee.*

In other words, what he's really saying is that sin is abounding more and more, and wherever you see sin, you see darkness, you see gross darkness, and darkness is covering this earth. Have you ever heard in the 70s, did you ever hear of the gross sins that you're hearing now? No, it's getting far worse, far worse, the things, the calamities that we are hearing, praise God, it's getting worse, far worse… gross darkness, gross darkness, blinding the minds.

We didn't have crack back then prominently like we have it today. There are different forms of wicked inventions that man is concocting in his mind, satan is injecting these wicked things in the mind, and man is taking what God has put in them, that ability to function and make things, but not for God's glory. They take God's glory and they make wicked inventions, evil inventions, and they're doing wicked things and their heart is getting that much harder and that much darker, but the Lord says gross darkness shall cover the earth, gross darkness.

That means even the light cannot pierce it except through God's people. The light out here is no light, all the education and the understanding that man is pertaining to, and getting understanding as far as how the body functions, what goes on. I see psychologists and psychiatrists on television just about every day saying what they have discovered, you know, in man, and still there's no answer, still there is no answer.

They're going through these things like a ritual, groping like blind people. There is no answer. They're spending billions of dollars to try to understand what's going on in the minds and in the hearts of mankind, and here's the answer, but they won't receive, they won't receive the light of the glorious gospel of Jesus Christ. Because he brings understanding, you see. They won't receive it. So what do they do? They continue to go to school, and they go and they go and they go and they spend fortunes and fortunes trying to understand how to live, and you know what they're doing? They're getting that farther and farther away from God, and the farther away from God they get, the more they grope darkness, the more they grope darkness, the more they cannot comprehend, so they just become lovers of themselves, and despisers of those that are good. Amen, Amen.

Thank God for education. Thank God, but my God, use it for the glory of God because education is of God. Did you know that? He is wisdom, He is knowledge, He is authority, and if you look at it, every man that's going after education, they think that it's to become that much more of an authority, you see. If you really look at it, and God is saying, I am the authority, and I am inviting you to share in my authority, but you reject the true authority and you go after your vain imaginations, see, and God is saying, if you're going to a higher education, glorify me in whatever you do. Glorify me.

This is why we are here on this earth. We are here only to bring glory and honor. He says, he commands us. Don't you know this is not just a petty little, come on, rise up and shine for me. Will you please? No, it's a command...Arise!

The more we see out here, the more you arise. The more you stand up for Jesus, the more you declare who he is, that he is the authority. He is the power, He is the purpose for living, but there is no life. No matter what we educate here, you see, if Christ is not ruling, it's no life. It's no life. Everything... this is what Paul did, he counted everything dung, but for the excellence of the knowledge of Jesus

Christ, that most excellent knowledge, he came to know, and he set out, he chucked it aside, all his learning. And Paul, the apostle, was a very learned man, see, very learned, but he set it aside. He counted it as nothing to go after the true knowledge, the true power, the true authority, and he found it.

And he cried out, Oh, to win Christ, because he saw the beauty of it all. He saw where the life was. It's in knowing who Jesus is, and Jesus does not want to hide himself in a mysterious cloud somewhere and not be revealed unto us. If that was the case, he would not have revealed himself after he rose from the dead to his disciples, you see. But no, he wanted the children of God to enter in, to who he is. Enter in, in the wisdom of God, in the knowledge, in the understanding, amen. And the Bible says that understanding is the wellspring of life. See, it's living.

You want to be wise, it's not how many scriptures you know. It's who wrote those many scriptures, see. You want to know the art of this book, and you'll find out, just like John, we call the Revelator, you'll find out that when he wrote, had they written every account of the acts that Jesus did, he said, I suppose the world could not contain it, amen.

That's how rich it is. That's how rich it is. And this is why what's left on record here, we go in it over and over, and we get something greater and greater and greater. Praise God in the highest. And this is what keeps us alive. It feeds our mortal being as well as our soul and our spirit.

I'm telling you the truth, because I knelt here today, just eating, eating the bread of life for not only my soul, but for my mortal body, amen, to be quickened and to be made whole, amen. When I got up this morning, the Holy Spirit just quoted the words of Christ, I am the Lord that healeth thee. And I said, Lord, I'm counting on it.

I'm counting on it. And I said, by faith, I receive it now, amen. So it was just easy to come in here and receive it. He could have done it there, but he waited till I got in the house of God, where all his people were, see, and when he starts pouring out whatever we have need of, your need may be different from mine. But as we reach out to him and give him the glory, I wasn't asking at that point to be healed, I'd already asked at home, you see, and here I am, made whole, and I feel strong in my body, where in the office, I'm trembling, praise God in the highest. God is a good God, amen. So let us honor the Lord in giving him the glory with our lips and with our hearts and with our lives, praise his holy name.

Then he says,

> And the Gentiles shall come to thy light, and kings to the brightness of thy rising.

See, the Lord has risen up on high, and his light is shining brightly or should be in the lives of his people, and when the Gentiles, that means those that are yet in darkness, praise God, see the glorious light. Now I'm using this in the spiritual sense, in the natural, I'll get back to this, but in the spiritual sense, we are spiritual Jews, we are the seed of Abraham, we are partakers of Jesus Christ.

The seed of Abraham means children of faith, okay, we know that the word of God says the just shall live by what? His faith, amen, those that are walking upright, doing justly in the sight of God, in the sight of God, shall live by the faith of God, alright. So just as Abraham, alright, Jesus is the offspring of that mighty faith that's given to us in this earth. Jesus came in a natural body, being the offspring of the natural body, see, but he is the faith that Abraham partook of.

You see this thing, Jesus said before Abraham was, I am, amen, do you see it? And the people said, What? what are you saying? You are not yet 50 years old, and how can you say that you were before Abraham? They didn't understand it, because they were abiding in darkness. You see, those that are in darkness do not comprehend what God is saying. That's why we've got to have life, dear ones, praise God, and he is our life. Okay, so if you hear me saying something that seems like I'm double-talking, I'm not really double-talking, it's just that Jesus has already said it, and like the children of old, they couldn't receive of him. And he had to talk to them in parables, and then when he would speak plainly, that would just baffle their minds, because they were children of darkness. Jesus said, You are the children of the devil, and he said, To you I speak in parables. Why? because they were not eager to know the greater things of God.

They were always trying to pick what Jesus said apart. We have people like that today. I had a visitor in my home this week, just like that. Trying to pick everything apart that was coming out of my mouth, and I was confronted with a very diabolical thing, really. This young man, only 19 years old, taken captive by a Haitian girl in her wickedness. Much older, I think she's in her 30s, and he'd come into a little fortune, and she just met him this Christmas, and grabbed that young man, and he said, he's hardly got anything left. And he said,

"But we're going to get married, this is my fiancé."

63

I let him talk, he insisted I get up out of my bed, and I said,

"No, talk to the ministers."

Because Pastor Wayne was down, and John. I said,

"You talk to them."

And he insisted on my being downstairs; he wanted to talk only to me, and I said,

"All right, he asked for it." and downstairs I went.

And as I sat there, he was telling me that he was, he said,

"Look, I'm just shaking. I just don't know which way to go, and I just told my fiancé, bring me by here."

I said,

"Where is she?"

And he said,

"Well, she went around to a friend's house, but she'll be back."

"That's all right." I said.

So I sat there patiently, and I let him, you know, pour out his heart, and when she came in, I knew it was time to speak. I said,

"I want you to get a Bible,"

And he, my son, got the Bible for him and her, and I opened up mine, and I began to read the Word of God, and I said, the Lord says, without the kingdom of God, are dogs, and sorcerers, and whoremongers, adulterers, and he that loveth and maketh a lie. I said,

"You understand what this means?"

And all of a sudden, the Holy Ghost conviction pricked her heart, and she began to use the scripture in a subtle, sneaky way; all I could see was a little serpent in her. I mean, he was actually moving just like this, in her, she didn't realize her body was swaying to that serpent, and I'm looking at this thing, and I'm seeing it, and my heart is grieved, because here, robbing the cradle, this 19-year-old youth, not even dry behind his ears. And she says,

"I'm gonna marry him."

I said,

"But I understand you... Didn't you say that you had a husband?"

Then she began to tell me what all the man had done to her, and so forth, and she said,

"You think God wants me not to be happy?"

I said,

'Oh yes, God wants you to be happy, just like He wants all the world to be happy, but we can only know happiness when we are at peace with Him. There is no peace to the wicked."

And I began to instruct them in the word of God, and satan, I began to realize that this young woman was really versed in the scriptures, and whenever she would say, You know, give a portion of God's word, I would take it a little bit further.

And she would say,

"God doesn't condemn anyone."

I said,

"No, He really doesn't, He convicts us of our sins, but we, because of our hellish ways, we condemn ourselves when God speaks the truth of us to us, and we despise this t ruth, the Bible says we love darkness rather than light, because our deeds are evil, we don't want God to disturb what we're doing, and therefore, we are in our own condemnation."

I said,

"Let me show it to you, since you're quoting the word, let's go further with it, amen." ...And this is how it went, praise God.

And then all of a sudden, I said,

"You are an adulteress.:

She said,

"But there was a woman that was caught in adultery, and Jesus forgave her."

I said,

"And He told her, Go and sin no more. Are you still sinning?"

She said,

"But I had a dream, and this old man in the dream told me to take care of him, watch over him."

I said,

"It's a lie from the pit! that's the devil talking to you. If God wants us to help anyone, He doesn't mean for us to grab that person and lie in the bed and wallow with them in sin, and adultery, and fornication."

I said,

"You are not born to get around God's word, young lady. You come in here, and you're copying scriptures; you had better be a doer of God's word, because God has brought you to the right place. I'm gonna give you the truth, amen."

I said,

"And I speak to you in the love of God, but you're not gonna come in here and be diabolical with God's word, and try to twist God's word in this young man's mind. I'm not gonna let you do it."

I said,

"Now what you do is your business, but I'll tell you one thing, since God has led you here, your blood is not gonna be on my hands, it's my desire as well as God's desire to see you set free. And let me tell you another thing," I said, "You are looking at one that the husband has left her, too." I said, "But look, out of God's goodness, I have raised these children in the name of the Lord my God, and I have not leaned on the arms of flesh. He told me not to go to the arms of flesh. He told me to trust the true and the living God."

I said.

"And you're saying that your children need a father, well then, you wait and trust God, turn your life over to Him, and pray! If God wants to turn your husband around, He'll turn him around; if He doesn't turn him around, bless God, God is able to be a father over your children!"

I took her to the book of Isaiah 54, chapter 54, and I said,

"You see what He says here, the Lord thy maker is thy husband," I said, "If husband walk out the door, let God Almighty walk in, and be a husband to you, and be a father to your fatherless children,"

I said,

"You've got no excuse, you just want to sin."

See, gross darkness overtaking the mind because of lust, and because of greed. And I turned to that young man, and I said,

"Young man, let me tell you something, your mother and your father... I have pleaded with down through the years."

He said,

"That's why I'm here, I know you would tell me the truth."

I said,

"Yes, I'm giving you the truth, but are you going to obey the word of God?"

He said,

"Miss Davis, I want to."

I said,

> "Well, let me tell you, you've got yourself bound up
> in something, young man…"

And what I was talking about was sorcery. I said,

> "You've got yourself bound up in something that
> only God can set you free from," I said, "That's an
> evil, and wicked young woman sitting there, and
> that's not your wife, she belongs to another man.
> You are caught in adultery because you have
> allowed yourself to be taken over by a woman."

I said,

> "And you're not even divorced from your husband,
> you're talking about marrying this young man, and
> you're not even divorced!" I said, "Even in the law
> of the land, you're not right!" It was a mess…

Now, I had to get up out of my bed and come down, and
preach this kind of thing, amen, and I'm going to do it, the
Bible says, arise, shine, for thy light is come. And this light
is telling the truth, and Jesus said, You shall know the truth,
and the truth shall make you free.

Glory to God in the highest! And I'm not ashamed of it,
because that God that I was talking about has been that
husband to my heart, amen. Has been that God to me in the
wee hours of the night, when I didn't know which way to
go, amen. And still is, when I don't know which way to go!
He's been that instructor to me, in the middle of the night,
when I didn't know what to do about problems,
surmountable problems, praise God in the highest!

I didn't have a husband to wake up and say, Honey, what do you think about such and such, but I can say, Father, what about such and such? What will you have me to do? Glory be to God in the highest, hallelujah, and he said, I'll be a father to your fatherless children, praise God, and I said, My God has helped me to raise them up, and everyone, all eight, praise God, have finished high school, and gone on to higher education.

I got two yet going, you know, to grade school, praise God in the highest, don't you tell me that God's not able. I said,

> "You are a liar from the pit!"

She said,

> "You calling me a devil?"

I said,

> "I'm calling you a child of the devil!"

…Amen, I said,

> "But God loves your soul, and I'm here to warn you that if you don't turn away from your wickedness, in hell you're gonna lift up your eyes."

> "I don't believe like you believe," she says.

I said,

> "Sister, let me tell you one thing, you don't have to, just keep breathing, praise God. This God that I'm talking about is gonna meet you one day, face to face, amen, hallelujah, my God, if that heart isn't right, in hell, you're gonna lift up your eyes, and you're gonna remember this night!"

70

Praise God in the highest, that's why I'm determined to speak the word of God, and live it, with all of my strength, and with all my heart! Because I know that whatever it's written here, it's gonna face me in the end. And I'm going to hear from my father, well done, thy good and faithful servant, enter thou end into the joy of thy Lord. Amen, praise God in the highest!

Don't be afraid to speak God's truth, don't be afraid, I don't care who it is, you know what satan brought to my mind? That's a Haitian and you know what they believe in... I said you can get all the voodoo's all the cuckoos and...I said I'm not afraid of you! I said it out loud, I said I'm not afraid of you, you foul devil! Amen. I know in whom I believe!

Praise God, I got the word of God again, and I tell you the word of God got so hot that that young lady got out. She couldn't stand it! She went outside and she started blowing the horn. And I said,

> "Young man, sit right here. I said that's the enemy trying to distract you." I said, "I'm not finished with you yet."

So he sat there, and all of a sudden she got out of the car. She came in the door, and I said,

> "Just come in and close the door."

She came in and she said,

> "Now let me... I just want to ask you one thing!"

I said,

> "NO! Don't ask me nothing! I'm talking to this young man, and I will not answer."

You see, I had given her time to prove what she was before she walked out that door, and what she really did was go out and try to get ammunition, and when she came back in, I was almost finished with the young man. And I said,

>"What I want to ask you, young man," I said, "will you let us pray for you? Because you are bound."

And he said,

>"Yes."

I said

>"You really will let us pray?"

And he said

>"Yes,"

I said

>"Get the anointing oil."

See, we anointed him, and I knew the work wasn't going to be done immediately, but the work is done! What I mean by that is, I knew with my natural eyes I was not going to see a change right there and then, but I know the work is done.

God did not send him by that house… nobody looks me up for nothing, glory be to God. They're too busy trying to run away, you see, because they know what they're going to get! And when God sends a young man out of the street to me, I know that I've got to be faithful to give him exactly what God sent him by to receive, and he received it. And he was telling her

>"Hush, hush, hush,"

You know, shut your mouth, and he was trying to get her, you know, to be respectful. I said,

"Never mind…"

And when I spoke in the authority of God, she held her peace and bowed her head. And she couldn't look, she just kept putting her hand over her head. Because I knew my eyes were looking right at her, and I knew Jesus had taken over! Praise God in the highest!

And I said

"I'm not afraid to speak the gospel to anyone, I don't care what your background is, I don't care where you're from, I'm gonna speak the truth. Because I know the truth is going to meet you in the end."
And I said, "You go on, you have your fling, but you're going to answer… you're going to answer to this God I serve! Amen."

God is true, and people think that, you know, because God is a merciful God, because he's good and he's long-suffering and he's kind and he's loving towards us, that we can do him any kind of way? Don't you know we have got to give account more to the mercies of God than the people of Nineveh? Jesus said so. Than the people of Sodom and Gomorrah? Because a greater than all of those patriarchs of old it's on the scene!

Amen, so we in this dispensation of an age of the Holy Spirit have got to give account… MORE SO! to what we do in our bodies, amen, than all the people under the law that died under the law, you hear me? That died out from the law, praise God, we've got to give account, precious ones, don't take this thing lightly because before, God winked at sin, he knew man was full of iniquity, Praise God, but no longer.

Because no person has the right to be full of sin today. God sent the perfect sacrifice, and His name is Jesus. Praise God, it's time to arise, it's time to shine. It's time to allow God to move in our innermost being, to embrace Him and to embrace everything that is spoken out of His mouth, embrace it, live by it! Do it! Do it with all your heart!

Praise God, but no longer because no person has the right to be full of sin today. God sent the perfect sacrifice, and his name is Jesus. Praise God. It's time to arise. It's time to shine. It's time to allow God to move in our innermost being, to embrace him, and to embrace everything that's spoken out of his mouth.

Embrace it. Live by it. Do it, do it with all your heart! He'll bless us with strength, He'll bless us with understanding. He'll bless us with the answers to our prayers. This is why I speak like I do. I said, my God, if I for one day fell to walk with God, honey, satan is waiting with all of his demons to flood my mind, to flood my home, to flood my children.

Praise God, and I love my children. A parent is not a real parent until they are in authority with Christ. Do you know that? We are not the stewards of God unless we are walking with God.
We are not in the full potential of parenthood unless we are walking with God. I see parents working their bones, just working this. I grew up, well, I finished growing up in the city of Newark, and I would see those parents putting all of these fine, expensive clothing on their children.

And I'd look at that, and I thought back on it many times since I've been saved. And all the finery that they had, and I mean they were dressed, going to school just like you see today. Fine clothing, expensive clothing, dressed up, going to get an education for their heads. And their heart is still out of tune with God. They're still out of beat with God, you see. And the parents enticing them to go on to their partying, go on to their reveling, go on to their banqueting, go on to the streets, live it up, to the games, revelings... going after all these things of the earth.

And yet, when you find the parents on a Sunday morning, where are they? The children just walk the streets, walk the streets on your way to the house of God. And you see the children somewhere playing so void, so void of their life, so void of their right, because the parents have no desire to know God. And they've got to give account for being bad stewards. They've got to give an account...

I remember when I was a little girl, this preacher woman that lived up on the corner from us used to come and plead with my parents to bring us to the house of God. And I would hear my mother saying, No, no, no. Every time, I'd stand up in the doorway and just listen. But in my heart, I wanted to go. And I wondered, why was Mama giving her so many excuses? Mama could take us.

And it was right up the hill, it was on the same street. But Mama said, No, the children can go after a while. And being reared Baptist at that point, we were still, you know, with my father, and he was Baptist. But this was a Pentecostal church. We didn't know anything about Pentecost. I was a little girl then. But this precious lady would come, and she said, Well, after they go to their church, can they come to ours in the afternoon? She said, We don't have Sunday school until 1 o'clock.

And my mother finally consented. And we'd go to our church. We'd go to our aunt's church, my mother's aunt's church, which was Presbyterian. And then we'd make it to the little Pentecostal church up on the hill. And that's where I learned that shooting marbles would lead to greater gambling. One sin adds on to another. How it looked so innocent. And then this preacher had drawn a picture of children playing marbles. And then he began to show the subtlety of sin. And bless God, I was shooting marbles like everything. I loved to shoot marbles. Anything that the fellows did, I thought I could do. And, you know, that grew up in the back of my mind. It was always there in my mind that if I do this, I'm going to gamble, I'm going to do this.

And he would show us how, later on, how they would ball up a dollar bill. He demonstrated it. And he said, when you see a person do that, they most likely will turn out to be a gambler. And I watched that thing, and God knows it's the truth. I've watched it down through the years. And, you know, as God blessed us to learn that, out of going all of those Sundays that we went to that Sunday school before we moved, it wasn't but a few months. But I learned more there than any Sunday school I had ever attended. You know why? Because they were getting to the heart of the matter. See that? And I remember those things.

And I have thought down through the years when I fell into wicked sin, sin after sin, before Jesus saved my soul. Had my mother not only sent me, but took me and then prayed with us, prayed with us, then that example, what a greater Christian I would have been long before Jesus saved me. I was saved at the age of 22, but I believe that knowing that I was chosen of God like I do now, I believe that had my mother been that living example of a good steward over God's children, that not only me, but my brothers and sisters would have long met Jesus Christ, long met Him.

Saints, it's important to live an upright life, to live a just life. And some are sitting in the house of God, and they're still bad examples. They lie, they cheat, they tell jokes on one another, play evil games, praise God, playing the lottery, and whatever, not trusting God to supply their needs, still evil stewards.

And God is telling Zion on the inside, this is why we come together, this is why we kneel before the Lord, that we might be clean from all of that filthiness, from all of that ungodliness, that we might be a true example, praise God in the highest, before our children. You know, God means for us to be a living example, and many, many mothers and many fathers are going to split hell wide open for the ungodly life that they are setting, the example that they are setting before their children. They want their children to do good, but they don't want to do good.

You see? And we're not glorying in these little ones; we are here to train them in the nature and the way of God. We don't glory in them, praise God, we want God's glory to shine upon them. If we want glory, let's see God in them, and because of the life that we are living before them.

You see? People wonder why the devil is running rampant in their homes. Praise God. God wants you to be an example of justice and righteousness, of peace, of love, real love, God's love, a God paid love, and that comes from only on high.

This is how we rise, this is how we shine, for the glory of the Lord is risen. Amen. Jesus has come, speaking in the natural now. I told you I'd get back to the natural part of this understanding. Let me read verse 3 again,

> *And the Gentiles shall come to thy light, and kings to the brightness of thy rising.*

When Jesus came to his own, only a few had received him. And because of that faithful few, because of those eleven, and the hundred and twenty, the glory of the Lord was risen upon Zion. And from that glorious and bright day that we call Pentecost, when the Holy Ghost was first poured out, and all those that were in Jerusalem saw the glory of the Lord upon those that had been filled with the Holy Ghost and fire. The word of God was spread abroad. Thousands were added, five thousand added to the church of the living God, the pillar and the ground of truth. Amen.

And from that day to this day, the glory of the Lord has risen. See? And because of those Jews, we Gentiles have shared in the brightness of his coming. And one day, Jew, Gentile alike, are going to behold him. We are going to see the glory of the Lord on a cloud, shining in the brightness of his glory, coming back for a glorified church, a church without sin, a church without spot, a church without wrinkle. Amen.

Pressed out. Amen. Through trials and tribulations, in the heat of the fire, pressed out. Praise God. Not sitting down on God. No time to get wrinkled. Amen. But on fire, bringing glory and honor to his name. And when he comes, precious ones, you know what we're going to be doing? We're going to be here glorifying him. And he's going to come to receive his glory that is upon us.

And if you read the book of Revelation, he said the kings of the earth shall bring their glory into the kingdom of God. Amen. That means whatever we have gained to bring honor to him on this earth, he's bringing it, and he's receiving it.

As we bring it, the Bible says we're kings and priests. Amen. You see, God is not looking at male or female. When he says kings and priests, he means the body of Christ. You understand this? God doesn't think or talk like man. He said Your ways are not my ways, neither are your thoughts my thoughts.

See, this is why it's important for us to be alive under him that we might be quickened to understand when he says kings and priests, that's us. Amen. Because in Christ Jesus, there's neither male nor female. But the Bible says we're all one. I'm quoting to you his word. See, look it up when you get home. Look it up. In Christ Jesus, there's neither male nor female, but we're all one. What? One spirit. See? In the eyes of God. And we kings and we priests of the earth will bring our glory into God's kingdom when we are caught up by Jesus, by the power of Jesus Christ. Amen.

Isn't it glorious? Thank God. Anyone that's not a Jew is a Gentile. Always remember that. If you're not a Jew, you're a Gentile. Yet, we are spiritual Jews. See? We're the children of faith. Making us the children of Abraham. Jesus Christ. Thank God. Thank God for Jesus. Being a Jew. Amen. Jews, you know, God knows what he's doing when he sent Jesus in the kinsmen of the Jews; the Jews have always been hated. Always will be hated. Always will be a rejected people. And God chose that which is most rejected, most unloved. Isn't that not like God? Amen.

To identify with. The love of God. The love of God came to a people that were so grossly hated. And still are, still are. Many times they have actually earned the hatred of other people because of their honory ways, because of their wickedness. You see? But God's promises are upon them. His blessings are upon them. His covenant is with them because of Abraham.

See? And no matter what you see, you look at what God says and align your heart right along with it. Don't you dare, don't you dare despise a Jew because he's a Jew. Because if you do, you're despising God who made that

Jew. Amen. You're despising God. And the glory of the Lord cannot rise upon you. Amen, Amen. No matter what you see them do, don't curse them in your heart. I don't care if they curse you; don't you curse them. You bless them and be blessed of God. Keep this ever in your mind and in your heart.

If you want God's favor upon you, if you want His blessings in this earth upon you, you bless that Jew. You bless Him. Bless Him with all your heart because you'll be doing yourselves a favor. Amen. Glory to God. I found that to be true. But if you truly want to bless the Jew, you gather your heart before God. Fast and pray for their salvation. Pray that their eyes will become open. See, their eyes are closed because we Gentiles had to come in. You see? But one day, one day, all Israel's eyes will behold the true Messiah. Okay, verse 4,

> *Lift up thine eyes round about, and see: all they gather themselves together, they come to thee: thy sons shall come from far, and thy daughters shall be nursed at thy side. Then thou shalt see, and flow together,*

This is what God is after. When we see, when our eyes are anointed to see what God wants to reveal to us. Oh, precious ones. Hallelujah. He said, Then we'll see. We'll see, and then we shall flow together. Together. That's what God is desiring of us.

To flow. Just like I hear Rory, you know, prompting you, you know, to get to Sunday school or to do certain things, you know, in the house of God. And just like the meeting was held, and things were presented to you to be a partaker of. And you know, you've been dragging your feet about these things. But see, that's not flowing together. That's not being laborers together.

You see, you're still out of harmony. You're still out of tune. You still haven't gotten a hold of your salvation. Glory be to God. This is the problem that Jesus had with the disciples. Their concern was about who was going to be the greatest. And who was carrying the money bag? And who was going to go and get the food to feed all of these folks? And we don't have enough here.

I mean, they were concerned about the secular things. It's like you're concerned today about your own things. And you have not made your heart rich towards God to be used to build His kingdom. To build His kingdom together in the elect of the earth. Praise God in the highest. And God is looking on, and He's saying you're not flowing yet.

My glory has not risen upon you yet. You're not quickened to understand who I am and what I'm after in you yet. Praise God. But when we begin to lay our ambitions aside and start putting our personal gain in the way of Jesus Christ, and count everything but dung for the excellent knowledge of Jesus Christ. Amen. And to do His good pleasure, not ours, His! Jesus didn't come to do His pleasure.

Had He come to do His pleasure, He would not have died. Amen. He would have just called all the 12,000 angels legions of them. Amen. Amen. Praise God. And fought the battle. And got out of here. But He said not my will, not mine. But thine be done. Praise God. And that's what we're going to have to learn. We're going to have to learn how to give our bodies a living sacrifice, precious ones. We're going to have to learn that God comes first in our lives.

Praise God. We're going to have to learn how to receive the true blessings of God. This is what we're going to have to learn if we are going to arise and shine for Him. We're going to have to learn how to put Him first. We're going to have to learn just like we get ourselves up and get to the marketplace, or get to the workplace, or get to the educational place. We're going to have to learn how to bring the same glory to God in the house of God.

He said the zeal of thine house hath eaten me up. And this is what's happening today. And I thank God. I just want to say this publicly. I thank God for you, Rory. I was just lying in the bed yesterday, and I said Lord, I thank you for that young man. You have given me some great young men. I was thinking of the one that God has raised up. Just like He kept killing those Soviet people off until He got a real leader to open up the Soviet Union to let His people, Jews, get out of there.

Praise God. God kept killing every leader that they would raise up. God knocked him off by the way of death. God did it. God said I kill and I make alive. Praise God. God killed him off. Killed him off. All three of them died until God got the one He wanted. His heart would be soft enough to yield to God and let God's people go. Amen. Amen. Glory to God in the highest.

And I saw God do the same thing up in Connecticut. Praise God. God brought down each pastor. He brought them down. He brought them down until God got the man that He wanted. Amen. Whose heart was yielded and whose heart was shed abroad in all the earth. I tell you that young man loves the souls in this world. You hear me? Glory to God. I tell you, it's marvelous just watching him. I marvel at him. I'm so thankful for that young man.

I was in the bathroom this morning early before anybody got up, and I was thanking God for that young man and I was thanking God for that young man and I was thanking God for that young man and I was thanking God for that young man. I mean, you carry a great place in my heart because I see the Lord molding you. Praise God, and how God just raised this one up when he was gallivanting out there in that world, didn't know which way he was going, groping about in darkness. Amen. And God took me out into a marvelous hotel. Glory be to God.

The Bonaventure Hotel in Los Angeles, California. Nothing but finery all around me, and you know where I spent that whole week? Had a fine room all alone, and I spent it on a towel on the floor, praying, seeking the face of God, seeking to know this great high priest in a greater way. Hours I'd spend in the presence of God at night, get up and shower, and go downstairs into a prayer meeting with thousands of other people.

Amen. Praise God. But I tell you on my way on my way home flying home God said a miracle awaits you when you get home and when I got home I mean not 10 minutes precious one when I got in that door threw my luggage up on my bed and was emptying out my bag I tell you my son walked through the door sat down by my bag and he said Mama he said I don't know about such and such one but I'm getting saved.

Praise God. And my mind went, I thought on that thing this morning, I said Lord, it was worth it. It was worth it to forfeit those great big beds, those nice comfortable beds, and stay on that floor, crying out to God to know him better. I just wanted to see Jesus in his glory in a greater way. Praise God in the highest. That's why I'm able to minister these things today.

This is why the revelations of God keep coming to me, because of those times that I spend on my face before God, pleading Lord, enlighten mine eyes that I might see you. I don't want to be some great preacher in the earth. I just want to declare who Jesus is, and I can't see him unless I go after him. Praise God in the highest. And to see the glory of the Lord upon this young man in the house of God, you know, with that zeal.

He always had zeal, always had zeal, and see that zeal being spent in the house of God. And I would tell him when he won the national achievement award, for the young businessman award over the nation, and he was showing me, you know, his plaques and the book and all of this stuff that they had given him, and you know, the recognition that they had given him because of his wisdom and stuff. And I said, he was wanting me to show more enthusiasm, and I said, Rory, I always knew that you were wise son. I always knew that, I knew that when you were two years old. I said, I'm happy for you, but you want me to truly be happy, son? I said, when I see that wisdom turned over to Jesus Christ, then I'll rejoice. Amen.

And I see it today, and I'm rejoicing. Praise God in the highest because this is where it's paying off. Serving the Lord. Serving the Lord. Glory to God. My God be glorified. And I told the Lord, I told him… about every one of them after I got saved. I said about all ten of them… Lord, I don't want to have anything that's not going to serve you. I'd rather that you take it now from my womb than me to birth anything in this world that's going to be a child of the devil. Amen.

And this is why you see them saved. This is why you see them, all of them in the house of God, except Valerie, and she tried to get here, but I made her stay home to rest her body. Because she's been going, and I knew she'd be here trying to sing, and you know she got sick all over again. And God gives us wisdom. Amen. When it's time to rest, it's time to rest.

And I said you rest your body. Praise God. But she would be willing to be here. She got up, went downstairs, got her clothing to get ready, and I said No, sister, you're staying home and you're going to rest that body. Amen. Glory to God because had I yielded to God and the understanding that he'd given me, she would be here today because she would have been already rested, and I praise God because it gave Michelle the opportunity to come and stand and bring God the glory through her singing through her yielding to God.

This is why we are here, and it's good to see how eager the young people are to serve the Lord. And sitting here playing the bells, the Lord gave me to know that he wanted the young people; he wanted to hear you sing. Amen. So dear ones, you get about your father's business and allow the Lord Jesus to strengthen you to sing for his glory.

Amen. You know it's something about the young what they do, I mean, they are in it means something to them. It's not just putting on a program, you know. I mean, it's in their hearts to yield, and God wants to hear it. Praise God in the highest. But this is what it's all about.
I'm not going to go any further in Isaiah 60. I just want to read this over again. Verse 4,

> *Lift up thine eyes round about and see.*

God wants you to look up and look around and take a good look and don't stop looking till you see what God wants you to see. Amen. And don't stop looking till you see what God would have you to see.

> *All they gather themselves together, they come to thee: thy sons shall come from far, and thy daughters shall be nursed at thy side. Then thou*

shalt see, and flow together, and thine heart shall
fear, and be enlarged.

Fear what? The terribleness of God. Fear the greatness of his power, holding him in great reverence. Praise God. Trembling because of who he is.

Have you seen people come to God, and all of a sudden, you just see them just trembling, or they be standing and trembling and seem like they have no control of their emotions, and they're trying not to show it, but they're trembling. It's because of the presence of God. Amen.

And then he says,

because the abundance of the sea shall be converted
unto thee, the forces of the Gentiles shall come unto
thee.

In other words, be soul winners. That's what he's really saying. Precious ones, be soul winners. God has given you one of the greatest ministries on the face of this earth to be a part of. We're out to win the multitudes from afar. We're out asking God for the heathen for our inheritance. What we have inherited from him, we're asking God for the heathen to inherit and for us to inherit them that God altogether might inherit us all. You see? This is what it's all about, and that means work.

That means lifting up our eyes and looking at the fields and seeing that they are already white to harvest. They are already ready to harvest, and if we don't see, it's because we haven't looked too clearly. Our eyes are yet on the face of this earth.

You see? We're seeing the things for ourselves, but if we would look around about and see, we'll see a people who are hungry for the truth. We'll see a people who are longing for the truth. This is why I tell you, I said, read these letters that come in here, that's coming from India, that's coming from the Philippines, that's coming from Africa, that's coming even from the States. And they are asking for literature, they're not asking for money, I am telling you the truth, they are not asking us for money, they're asking for the Word of God.

They're asking for literature, pamphlets, cassettes…this is what they're asking for mainly. And they are asking for our prayers, that God may enrich them to get into a good Bible school, to get into the house of God. That the Lord may build churches for them, this is what they're asking for. That they might win their countries to Jesus Christ. How much do you value it? How much do you really care about where God has placed you? Have you truly indeed arisen? Is the light of God surely shining brightly?
Praise God, how many are lingering before God, when others get up off the altar, and are praying these requests through? How many are sobbing for those yet abiding in darkness all around about us that are full of drugs, full of crack, full of murder, full of perversion? See? Full of the devil! Amen!

How many are pleading with those that are in darkness? How many are pleading with God and asking God for mercy on their lives, that they won't die in darkness and go to Hell? After I told that young woman the truth, and that young man, when she went out the door, I said, Dear one, I still hold to God's Word, but I love you. I want you to know, I love you, and I'll be praying. Amen! And she went out hating me, she went out hating God in me, Praise God. But I know one day…and the Lord gave me to know that those words will follow both of them, that they have no rest, no rest, no rest because God sent them to hear the truth.

You see the love of God? You see the mercies of God? Amen, and whether you see them coming to God or not, give them the truth, give them the truth. Don't say how am I gonna do it? Or, I don't want to hurt their feelings, honey, you hurt their feelings and get their souls saved.

JESUS IS ALIVE AGAIN

First Aired March 31ˢᵗ, 1991

The fifth chapter of the book of Hebrews. Do you have the scriptures while you're looking? I just want to say, I thank God for my daughter coming in. I got a lot of them. This one is coming in from Tennessee. I was just talking about her the other day to a friend of mine from Connecticut. I was telling him how, when God first started us here in the ministry of intercessory prayer in Montclair, we were in my home, and we would work sometimes around the clock in intercessory prayer. And the Lord would fill our living room from one space to the other.

I mean, the seats would all be taken, so that people would just sit on the floor, and then they started filling up the dining room. And then they started filling up the staircase, and then they started filling up the kitchen until the parents began to find out that it was prayer going on. And one in particular, we prayed all night long.

She left around one or one-thirty because she had a curfew, she had to be at home, she was a teenager. And I had gone into the kitchen to get just a glass of water, and as I'm standing there pouring the water to drink, I see this bike ride up and I looked and it was this one that he left around one 30, she was back again around six o'clock, almost six o'clock am to get in on the last phase of prayer.

And, namely, that was Linda sitting in our midst from Tennessee. She went off to college, and she forgot to come back home. So periodically she'll come and bless her, bless us with her presence, and we thank God because she's still holding on to the faith of Jesus Christ.

And I'll never forget, there are many things, many things we've seen God do here in Montclair, but certain things just stand out in that. I marveled standing there at that sink. I said, Lord, she's willing to suffer ridicule and whatever, to be here in prayer. Slipped out of her bed, I know she slipped out, supposed to be going for a ride on her bike, but she was riding to 39 James Street to be in prayer, and we weren't partying, we weren't, we weren't partying in the world.

We were in the presence of God, and that's what her soul longed for. And God filled that place; there were Jews, there were Italians, there were blacks, there were Hispanics, you name it, it was in the midst. And most of them were teenagers looking for an answer. And Montclair is a very rich place. Mostly the middle class in our area and the poor. But Montclair somehow has had such a sense of pride, and this is what we had to pull down here.

We had to encounter a sense of pride that was not a normal thing. It was beyond what we had ever experienced in any town, anywhere God had sent us.

And because of that, it was a turn-off just to have payer service in the home, but God said, Start it, and that we had to do. And then the parents started showing up to find out what's going on here and which was good. That showed us they did care.

But when they begin to come and they begin to see the difference in their children, some don't want their children to live a wholesome life. They would rather that they be out doing whatever... than to be in prayer.

And one minister came by because his flock would go to church on Saturday, but they'd end up at our place on Wednesday night, and he just couldn't understand what could be in this little house that is carrying my people away. So he decided to come by, and that he did one night. Sad to say, God gave me great grace, but he withstood the power of God, and God would not permit it.

And the Lord told me to go and tell him to get on the altar himself, on his altar at his church, and the congregation alike. And he said, he won't hear you, but go and tell him anyway. And he said, after you deliver my word, get out of there.

And he also warned him that if he didn't obey, God would bring judgment. So the folks begin to slowly see that I didn't come to Montclair to steal their sheep, but to work with them. But where they would not allow the Holy Spirit to work, God kept 39 James Street in reserve... that he did.

And one year later, because the pastor withstood the message of God and the messenger, he didn't realize that it was God that sent me. And one year later, God put him in his grave. I didn't pray it, it was a shock to me, like to anyone else. The Lord didn't tell me what he was going to do. He just told me to go and deliver his word, and his sheep kept right on coming. Amen. So it's very important to not take God lightly. He is to be revered. He is to be honored.

He is to be obeyed because we are just about to go into the Word and see why God is to be honored and not to be taken lightly. Hebrews four verses 14 and 15, I'll read,

Seeing then that we have a great high priest, that is passed into the heavens, Jesus the Son of God, let us hold fast our profession. For we have not an high priest which cannot be touched with the feeling of our infirmities; but was in all points tempted like as we are, yet without sin.

There've been many movies, many lies, blasphemies, gone up against the purity and the holiness of the Son of God, but it's all lies.

Jesus yet remained without sin. Although he was tempted with every sin that satan has tempted mankind throughout the ages, but Jesus kept himself pure by the power of God.

Let us therefore come boldly unto the throne of grace, that we may obtain mercy, and find grace to help in time of need.

That means in our hour of temptation, when we need him the most, he says, Come boldly to the throne of grace. Chapter five,

For every high priest taken from among men is ordained for men in things pertaining to God, that he may offer both gifts and sacrifices for sins: who can have compassion on the ignorant, and on them that are out of the way; for that he himself also is compassed with infirmity. And by reason hereof he ought, as for the people, so also for himself, to offer for sins.

He's speaking of the Old Testament age.

And no man taketh this honour unto himself, but he that is called of God, as was Aaron. So also Christ glorified not himself to be made an high priest; but he that said unto him, Thou art my Son, To day have I begotten thee. As he saith also in another place, Thou art a priest for ever. After the order of Melchisedec.

Who in the days of his flesh, when he had offered up prayers and supplications with strong crying and tears unto him that was able to save him from death, and was heard in that he feared; though he were a Son, yet learned he obedience by the things which he suffered;

And we know that Jesus went into the garden of Gethsemane. There, Judas led Roman soldiers to take Jesus as he was offering himself in prayer, crying unto God. All the miracles that he had performed, all the healings that he had brought, all the mighty good works that Jesus had manifested, and the mighty word that he had taught and preached. His work was ending, but he had one mighty work to do.

And that was the whole sum of the matter in manifesting the power of God, through the power of the Holy Spirit, was to go to that cross and die. And we know that his dying was not readily accepted by Jesus Christ. He knew his whole purpose in coming. Yet when that time was approaching, Jesus began to be grieved in his spirit, heavy in spirit because he was not going to that cross to die for a few people. He was going to that cross to taste death for every man everywhere. And that was a heavy burden.

That was not an easy task. For one person to die for all the world, to take upon himself, that pure Holy body, soul and spirit, the sins of the entire world... It's very, very heavy. And to contemplate that, to just think ahead of what was nearing, his purpose in coming became almost too much to bear in the physical.

And this is why Jesus was found in the garden of Gethsemane crying out his soul unto God as, as great sweats of blood, drops of blood pouring out his pores... tears, sweat and blood, water and blood for our sakes. Knowing that he had to do it, knowing that everything that he had done had led up to this moment. So he's in the garden preparing himself, and then comes the one that betrayed him. He said he didn't choose to be a high priest.

Hebrews five, verse four and five,

> *And no man taketh this honour unto himself,*

Anybody in their right mind. This is why you see people today running from that office of proclaiming the gospel of Jesus Christ because it's a lot to pay.

> *And no man taketh this honour unto himself, but he that is called of God, as was Aaron. So also Christ glorified not himself to be made an high priest;*

Christ didn't do it. It was the will of the father,

> *but he that said unto him, Thou art my Son, To day have I begotten thee.*

It was God, the father.

> *As he saith also in another place, Thou art a priest for ever After the order of Melchisedec. Who in the days of his flesh, when he had offered up prayers*

and supplications with strong crying and tears unto
him that was able to save him from death,

That's the reason he was in that garden. He wanted God, the father, who was able to spare him from death… to spare him. This is why he cried, Father, take this cup from me.

The cup of dying, the cup of death, death to his body… sufferings before the death, untold sufferings. We will yet learn in the future, when Jesus brings us home, what all he suffered for us. We're only seeing in part, we only hear in part, we read in part, but we are going to know when we behold his face in glory, we are going to know what Jesus went through for our sakes, but that, that we know in part, embrace it.

The light that God gives us of his son, embrace it! Don't let it go. Verse eight,

> *though he were a Son, yet learned he obedience by*
> *the things which he suffered; and being made*
> *perfect, he became the author of eternal salvation*
> *unto all them that obey him;*

Jesus became the author of our salvation. He's the author of our faith. Whatever we believe concerning the report that is written of Jesus Christ, Jesus is the one who has authorized faith in us to become active, because we believe. Jesus is

> *called of God an high priest after the order of*
> *Melchisedec. Of whom we have many things to say,*
> *and hard to be uttered, seeing ye are dull of*
> *hearing.*

…many things to say, but the verse that stood out to me,

and being made perfect.

Verse nine, Jesus being made perfect while in a fleshly tabernacle, while in a physical body like you and me, because he dared to follow God all the way. He dared to obey every step, every order, every command, every will of God.

Jesus said, Nevertheless, not my will but thine be done. He willed to escape the impending sufferings on that cross and death and hell, but he knew his father's will. Is that not like us? Many times, we dread to do what we know God is requiring. But yet we submit ourselves to God's divine and high order of command, because obedience works peace. It brings peace between God and man. And God did this for our sins while we were yet sinners. No one can take Christ's glory.

All that we do, all the work that we perform, could never measure up to what Jesus has done, but God did not choose any other being. He chose his only begotten son, and only that begotten son could get the job done of bringing salvation to the world, to mankind. He didn't sit in the heavenlies and wait for us to come up unto him.

He came down. He was made lower than the angels that ministered unto him in his glory, and he took on himself earthly form that he might know and feel what we go through. That no man could accuse God in the day of judgment and say, But you didn't know you could not understand why I did these things against you.

We can never say that to God because God sent his son, and he took on himself the form of flesh. What we feel, he feels what we have suffered. He already had.

Jesus was tempted by satan, ordered by the Holy Ghost to be tempted by demons and satan himself, that we would be without excuse. And Jesus withstood him, withstood the enemy by saying, It is written, it is written, giving us a perfect example to say also in the hour of temptation, satan, it is written. The word of God says that when satan tried to tempt the Lord Jesus Christ, he let him know! This is God you're coming against, for the word of God says, thou shalt not tempt the Lord by God.

And he was not afraid to say that he was equal with God the Father because God was his father on earth. Amen. Indeed, he was born of a Virgin Mary, but the Holy Spirit brought conception to her womb. A Spirit that is holy, pure. We glory in Jesus Christ today. We glory in his name, but there is no other name.

Hebrews chapter seven. We'll begin at verse 22

> By so much was Jesus made a surety of a better
> testament.

not like the other priests of old in the Old Testament age, but Jesus was made a surety of a better Testament, a new Testament.

> And they truly were many priests, because they were
> not suffered to continue by reason of death:

There were many because they kept dying and someone else had to take their office, you see, but no one can take

Christ Jesus' office. He's the only great high priest that ever lives to make intercessions for the saints.

But this man,

verse 24,

because he continueth ever,

He's alive!

hath an unchangeable priesthood.

Death couldn't swallow him up. Death couldn't hold him in satan's dominion because when his spirit left the body, it went down to hell to destroy the power of satan in hell, that is. Not only on the face of the earth when he gave his life a ransom for all mankind. Being mocked, being ridiculed, being scorned, blasphemed...

Devils and men rejoiced in glee because they thought they had him. There he is, we've got him. We stopped his good works from interfering with our dominion over mankind, and they rejoiced. They, called from one part of the earth to the other. Come and rejoice.

We've got him! Right where God allowed them to put him. That all men everywhere might have a right to life itself, because without the shedding of blood, there is no remission of sin.

Jesus called his disciples unto him and he said, Whosoever sins you remit, they are remitted. Whosoever sins you retain, they are retained. This is after Jesus had risen from the dead, and he's given man those that love him. Those who were chosen by God unto him. He was giving man the authority and the power of his Holy name.

To operate in that same power, that same authority, that same grace by the same Holy Spirit whom we know is the Holy Ghost, that mighty comforter, that sealer, the spirit of truth, the wisdom of God.

Jesus Christ called his disciples to him and gave them to know, You go into all the world and you preach that I'm alive.

You see, I called you unto myself because some of you doubted I might be alive. You doubted Mary Magdalene's testimony that she saw me. You doubted me. So here I am. Come here, Thomas. You said you would not believe unless you saw the nail prints in my hands, unless you thrust your hand in my side. Come, here I am. While the door bolted not only shut but locked.

Jesus walks through, and he still does some of you were coming in, and we were singing. Come in the room. Come on, Jesus will meet you, the Holy Spirit will greet you, and he does. Amen.

Wherever Jesus is lifted up, the Holy Spirit is there to enlighten us, to empower us to believe, and to become a partaker of life itself of heaven. Amen. We're physically here, but I don't know about some of you Christians, I don't, I don't know. I can't answer for you, but many times I'm here. This body is, but my soul and spirit are soaring under the heavenlies because the Bible says we sit in heavenly places.

No, it's not astral projection. It's that we are caught up in the spirit by the spirit of God to behold marvelous things, wondrous things. How do you think the Bible is written? The apostle Paul said, I was caught up in the spirit, up in the heavens. I don't know if it was a third heaven or where I don't know where I was. And he said, I saw marvelous things, which is unlawful to utter. God... giving revelation of his Holy presence. I'll show you later. Let me read 22 again.

> *By so much was Jesus made a surety of a better testament. And they truly were many priests, because they were not suffered to continue by reason of death: but this man, because he continueth ever, hath an unchangeable priesthood. Wherefore he is able also to save them to the uttermost that come unto God by him, seeing he ever liveth to make intercession for them.*

Jesus is interceding for us. Why? Because he left us here in a world that is yet run by the devil. Christians are here combating the evil forces of hell that are running loose on earth.

But Jesus said, Be of good cheer, in this world you shall have tribulation, but be of good cheer, for I have overcome the world. So we're ever looking unto Jesus. He ever lives to see us through prayerfully, and we're ever looking unto Jesus while we are here because he's the author and the finisher of our faith. What he began in us, he's going to finish it. As a matter of fact, it's done already.

The way God operates, he sees the end from the beginning, and to every Christian that operates in faith, we know that we shall see Jesus in peace because he is the author of our faith. We believe the report given. Isaiah asked of old, Lord, who has believed our report and unto whom is the arm of the Lord revealed. God said he would lay bare his arm of salvation, and God does.

When he reached down and picked us up, he was laying bare his arm to go down to the pit of sin and deliver us from ourselves, the world, and the devil.

For such an high priest became us, who is holy,

Verse 26, he's holy,

> *harmless, undefiled, separate from sinners, and made higher than the heavens; who needeth not daily, as those high priests, to offer up sacrifice, first for his own sins, and then for the people's:*

He doesn't need to do that,

for this he did once, when he offered up himself.

He only had to die once, just once. That's the power of our testimony. Lord, we believe… In St. John, He said the world cannot receive because they don't believe. And no man can come to him unless they believe, and no man can believe unless they are the property of God. That's how God operates. Faith, not by sight… faith.

Many say I don't believe. That's nothing new. There's nothing new under the sun. Many before you did not believe. Jesus said you're your father, the devil. He's a liar from the beginning. He lies to the children of men and tells them that it's not true. And yet he trembles because he knows it is.

And this is a marvel to me, and it's ammunition for me. I marvel that one who was made, created so beautiful and empowered with such might and authority to be in the presence of God Almighty, could rise up against his maker, against his creator, and say I'll be like the Most High God.

He knew he couldn't be him. So he said I'll be like him. He sealed his doom right there. And it was just a matter of moments before he was cast out of heaven. Moments, just moments as far as God's concerned.

And this is where the war between mankind and God, and satan began because he was cast out of heaven, defeated and rendered powerless in heaven. All the power and authority that he had became corrupt and still is, and it's getting worse, far worse. Verse 28,

> *For the law maketh men high priests which have infirmity; but the word of the oath, which was since the law, maketh the Son, who is consecrated for evermore.*

Only Jesus, the great high priest, has performed that mighty work. Hebrews chapter 9, verse 11,

> *But Christ being come an high priest of good things to come, by a greater and more perfect tabernacle,*

Remind you, Jesus Christ was made perfect through the things which he suffered.

> *But Christ being come an high priest of good things to come, by a greater and more perfect tabernacle, not made with hands, that is to say, not of this building; neither by the blood of goats and calves,*

which the priests used of old

> *but by his own blood he entered in once into the holy place,*

Once it's emphasized by the Holy Ghost

having obtained eternal redemption for us. For if
the blood of bulls and of goats, and the ashes of an
heifer sprinkling the unclean, sanctifieth to the
purifying of the flesh: how much more shall the
blood of Christ, who through the eternal Spirit
offered himself without spot to God,

He was without spot, without sin, without stain, without blemish, and he offered through the power of the Holy Spirit himself to God!

purge your conscience from dead works to serve the
living God?

We have a conscience, every man. God has put it in us. It tells us when we're right and when we're wrong. It convicts us when we override the right that we know to do. That's the conscience of man. And this is how God deals with us. This is how the doors of our hearts are open unto God. It's through our consciousness. Amen.

Now the blood of Jesus was shed to purge our sins away from that which we know we're guilty of. Our conscience bears witness against us or for us. When the preaching of the word comes, our conscience acknowledges in us that we are guilty or that we are clean, and it's all due to the blood of Jesus Christ. It's not that Christians don't hear, it's just that as the word of God comes…it's by water by the word and by the blood, when the word of God is being proclaimed, our conscience gives us to know the right or the wrong that's in us.

If it's right, the heart says yea, amen. If we're wrong, the Lord says repent, and the conscience bears witness that there's a need to repent of our guilt of our wrong. God doesn't accuse us. He comes to help our infirmities. This is the whole reason Jesus came to deliver us from the guilt of our consciousness of right or wrong with his blood and his blood purges.

All we have to do is ask in his name, just ask Lord thy word has found me guilty. I ask your forgiveness for this wrong or this sin, that you and your word have proclaimed to me today. And the blood is in motion immediately purging, washing away the guilt and the stain and delivering us from spots and blemishes.

This is how the Saints are going to go into God's kingdom and through those pearly gates without spot, the blood and the word and the water that have purified us continually... continually!

This is why it's necessary to be in the house of God continually that we might hear the preaching of the word, and if we're straight, we remain upright, and if we are not, we repent and become upright by the power of God's word and the power of the blood and the water. Amen, the Holy Spirit is that living water. Isn't it marvelous the plan of God, the salvation that God has wrought for us through Jesus Christ?

This is Easter, and every Christian lives with this on their minds and in their hearts and in their souls, and this is why we live and breathe, we rise up and we lie down, we walk through the day. Whatever we're doing. He's on our minds and on our hearts, and we're not religious fanatics. It's our life! He's our lifeline, and whatever we do, whatever we say, we want to bring glory to God even as Christ did.

It's marvelous, the plan of salvation, the reason Jesus came and the reason he died and the reason he rose again from the dead and ever lives. He's alive. Hallelujah.

Verse 13

> *For if the blood of bulls and of goats, and the ashes*
> *of an heifer sprinkling the unclean, sanctifieth to the*
> *purifying of the flesh: how much more shall the*
> *blood of Christ, who through the eternal Spirit*
> *offered himself without spot to God, purge your*
> *conscience from dead works to serve the living*
> *God?*

From dead works, if it's dead, bury it, amen. Amen if your
works are not bringing glory to God, bury them, to serve
the living God, God's alive!

> *And for this cause he is the mediator*

Verse 15,

> *of the new testament, that by means of death, for the*
> *redemption of the transgressions that were under*
> *the first testament,*

Every man was ordered to die; every man was doomed to
die in trespasses and sins under the law, under the old order,
under the Old Testament. You ever wondered why the word
of God says the Saints… When Jesus rose from the dead,
the Saints got up out of the graves and walked and were
seen of many in Jerusalem. He didn't say that all the people
who had died were seen only the Saints.

Why? Because every man was doomed to die, and they
were held in a holding camp. You might say in Hades, the
good and the bad, until Jesus came. This is why it was
important for Jesus to go to hell to take the keys of death to
take them.

He didn't go and order satan to hand them over. He took them on satan's Dominion in Hades, and he unlocked the prison doors in hell. And said Saints be loosed, be free go home. Hallelujah. Now it is not written that the Saints tarried to talk to any Christian that was alive. The Christians just happen to see them passing to paradise.

Don't get caught up in necromancy; it is of the devil. Amen. The Lord allowed the Christians to witness the resurrection of those that had died in the law. That kept the law that they might know that there is life through Jesus Christ. Martha said Lord, if I had been here, Lazarus, my brother, would not have died.

Jesus, let him know, let her know, mother. I am the resurrection. He didn't wait till he went to the cross. He said I am, I am now. All the while I'm standing here, Martha. I'll show you I'm life everlasting, and not only am I life, but I am part life. He said Do you believe this? Do you believe Martha? She said Lord. I know that you shall you shall raise him up in the last day. He said Martha, I am.

I am every day. You are governed by days, Martha, but I am everlasting. I'll prove it to you. Lazarus, come forth! And here comes Lazarus bound in grave clothes, and Jesus said Loose him, unwind him, and let him go. Freedom, body, mind, and soul. And everybody believed for that moment? For that moment, but how quickly man forgets? How quickly? This is why we have to get him on the inside.

What we see on the outside. We will forget satan will work on us and work on us and mesmerize our minds. Tell us all none of that really wasn't that you that was just you were just hallucinating.

This is why Jesus said If my word abides in you and you in me... twofold. In, safely in, no man can take it from you, and satan can't take it out of you. Amen. Let me read for 15 again,

> *And for this cause he is the mediator of the new testament, that by means of death, for the redemption of the transgressions that were under the first testament, they which are called might receive the promise of eternal inheritance.*

Ask yourselves, has he knocked on your door? Are you called? Did you answer? Did you give your life over to the resurrection and life? Is he with you? It's his will...

He said for many,

> *They which are called might receive the promise*

Not only called, but to receive.... Jesus said in another portion of Scripture Many are called, but few are chosen, many will not receive him, and that's where they stop. This is the difference between the called and the chosen. The chosen accepts what he says and receives him, but the called believes but stops right there.

You go in the streets, you deal with the homeless, and so forth, and you cannot tell those people that they don't believe, and some have had beautiful experiences in being called unto God, but they didn't stay with him. We must receive him.

Every word that comes out of his mouth. We must receive. It's life. The Word of God is life. Everlasting. Bless his Holy Name.

For where a testament is, there must also of necessity be the death of the testator. For a testament is of force after men are dead: otherwise it is of no strength at all while the testator liveth. Whereupon neither the first testament was dedicated without blood.

For when Moses had spoken every precept to all the people according to the law, he took the blood of calves and of goats, with water, and scarlet wool, and hyssop, and sprinkled both the book, and all the people, saying, This is the blood of the testament which God hath enjoined unto you. Moreover he sprinkled with blood both the tabernacle and all the vessels of the ministry.

Now Israel, they would come up on this high and holy day for remission of their sins that they committed all through the year or throughout the year. And when they came, there were goats and lambs and turtle doves and whatever animal slain. And they would take the blood of those animals and sprinkle. The high priest would sprinkle the people with the blood. He would sprinkle himself with the blood. He would sprinkle the altar with the blood.

I mean blood… of animals! And those animals had to be without spot. They had to be perfect or else it could not be accepted. And yet man kept right on sinning, right on sinning. And God had to choose a better way, that this thing would be done once and for all. That man would stop sinning and be conscious, completely conscious of the fact that he belongs to God and God belongs to him.

No more darkness, no more blindness, no more hardness, but completely walking in the light and being illuminated by the Spirit and the power of the Holy Ghost. God had to put a stop to this; it became a ritual. And that's the way mankind is. He'll get accustomed to doing certain things a certain way, and you can't move him. He's gonna do it that way, that's the way he learned it, and that's the way it's gonna be. And this is why God had to choose a new and better way.

And had not Jesus come and had not Jesus gone to that cross, had not his hands been pierced and the blood of thorns springing down his face, his side pierced, his feet pierced, his body beaten and swollen, and his face marred and swollen. Beaten to a pulp, you might say, that every part of his being from his head to his feet, every part of his being… bleeding! For our sakes. He had to die for our sakes. That was the ultimate offering for man's sin, ours.

We can't forget it. The Holy Spirit will not permit us to forget. Our salvation will be doomed if we dare forget. This is why man commits sin, because they are not consciously aware that that sin has already been paid for. And God is not to be taken lightly for the payment of our sins.

And we are indebted. We say, well, I didn't ask him to die. Children say to their parents, I didn't ask you to have me, I didn't ask to be born. But the fact is, you are. And the fact is, we were born sinners. And the fact is, that sinner's going to die. And the fact is, when that sinner dies, there's judgment. And after judgment, there is the destiny…Hell. And not in a holding camp, but hell and fire.

So, this is why God sent his son to redeem us from the power of sin, hell, and the grave. And this is why we sing, up from the grave he arose. And Jesus asked hell, and he asked death, Where's your power to hold me? And death, where's your sting? You couldn't touch me, for I am incorruptible. I am life eternal.

No man, he made it very clear, can take my life. I lay it down on myself. He did it in obedience to the Father. And he said, if I lay it down, I shall take it up again by the power of the Holy Ghost. Jesus took his life up. The Holy Spirit never forsook him.

He was right there all along, followed him right on down into hell. And when the work was accomplished in hell, the saints were loosed, the keys taken, that satan would have no power over us on this earth, and he doesn't. He attacks us to make us think that he's powerful, but he is cast down. The word of God says so, I believe God.

And if we get raked over and knocked over, it's not because God is telling satan to do it to us. It's that we are not taking into consideration that that is done for us, and coming into our inheritance with Jesus Christ. We have inherited all things that heaven can offer. Amen.

When I was sick, I lay there thinking on everything that Jesus had brought to my remembrance that he had done for me. And I was determined, Lord, you are my resurrection, you are my life, you are my healer, you are my health, you are my prosperity. And I began to name those things, and I began to name them to me, myself. And then I began to turn those things on the enemy.

And I said, This is mine, you're here to steal it from me, but no, no. And the enemy was telling me to prepare to leave here, get my insurance, and get all of this in order. See, he wanted to steal my mouth.

He wanted me to stop picking on him and stopping him where he's fighting God's people. And I said, No, I'm not going to die, not at all, no way. Not me! God's not ready for me. No, uh-uh, death, get out of here. And I literally stood up in my bedroom and I kicked him.

In Jesus' name, I said, you get the hell out of here. I'm alive. And I threw up my hands and I said, Lord, I bless you for life. And from that day on, I began to mend. All the while I'm lying there, and I'm weighing this out and wasting time. And this is what the Lord was telling Martha, I am the resurrection, enter in, Martha, enter in by faith, believing. Do you believe? Yeah, Lord, I believe in the last day. Martha, I Am.

The last days are in the future... I am, is now. Amen. And this is why we can go around telling folks, God can do it. He'll do it. Don't you believe? Come on, let's believe. Let's believe. If you believe, I'll pray the prayer of faith. You don't even have to manifest; just let me believe with you. Amen.

And God gets the work done. He's so eager, not only to give us life, but to manifest miracles in our lives. Yes, he is! But it's up to us to believe the word. I'll continue, let me go to 22 again,

> *And almost all things are by the law purged with blood; and without shedding of blood is no remission.*

Without the shedding of blood, there is no remission of sins.

> It was therefore necessary that the patterns of things in the heavens should be purified with these, but the

heavenly things themselves with better sacrifices than these.

For Christ is not entered into the holy places made with hands, which are the figures of the true; but into heaven itself,

That's where Christ is. This is where he's entered.

now to appear in the presence of God for us:

Isn't this marvelous that he's there on our behalf? He's our mediator. Amen. Standing between God and ourselves. This is why no man can come to God except through Jesus Christ. He said it on the right hand of the Father.

And all we got to do is use the power of attorney. His name, his name is given to every man that believed, every person that believed the name of Jesus can get us. Yay and amen. The inheritance of God's kingdom. See, this is restoration. Jesus brought restoration. Mankind lost their inheritance when Adam and Eve were cast out of the Garden of Eden because of satan, satan's a thief.

He stole the birthright; Jesus Christ brought it back. And not only did he give us the birthright, but he gave us access to heaven itself, not the garden of Eden, but heaven.

And we can enter into God's holy presence anytime we choose. Because we come in Jesus' name, recognizing, acknowledging, and speaking unto God through Jesus Christ. Why him? Because he is the only one that gave his life.

And God means for us to honor that, that Christ Jesus has done. We must honor him. No man can come to God unless Jesus Christ rules in our minds.

Turn with me to St. John chapter 11. I'll quickly go through these scriptures by God's grace. St. John chapter 11, verse 25, I'll begin to 27. This is Jesus answering, as I stated more than once. Jesus answered Martha concerning her brother Lazarus.

> *Jesus said unto her, I am the resurrection, and the life: he that believeth in me, though he were dead, yet shall he live:*

He that believeth in me, and we know Lazarus believed. He loved Jesus Christ.

> *and whosoever liveth and believeth in me shall never die. Believest thou this?*

Whosoever believeth in me shall never die? Whosoever? Whosoever?

> *She saith unto him, Yea, Lord: I believe that thou art the Christ, the Son of God, which should come into the world.*

And that's exactly what God is desiring that we say unto him. When we come in his presence many times, you just sing because you don't know what to say. So, because of the ignorance or the lack of knowledge of the power of God's word, you just sing something or say amen and really don't know what you're doing. But if we answer Christ like Martha answered him, she said

> *Yea, Lord: I believe that thou art the Christ, the Son of God, which should come into the world.*

And when she acknowledged her belief openly, she got action. She got action.

And when she had so said, she went her way, and
called Mary her sister secretly, saying, The Master
is come, and calleth for thee

And we saw what Jesus did. Jesus said, I got a faith stirred.
I got her to acknowledge her faith openly.

Now we don't know any other portion of scripture where
Martha confessed openly unto Jesus that she believed he is
the Christ that should come. How did she hear this? The
prophets of old. She was well read, she looked for the
Christ. And when he stood there full of life itself, she
acknowledged what she saw and what she believed. And
she got her brother raised again from the dead. Marvelous,
isn't it? St. John 17, verses 1 through 3,

These words spake Jesus, and lifted up his eyes to
heaven, and said, Father, the hour is come; glorify
thy Son, that thy Son also may glorify thee: as thou
hast given him power over all flesh,

Over all flesh…God the Father gave Jesus Christ, the Son,
power over every one of us. But he is so gracious and such
a gentleman that he will not force his power upon any of
us, like the other fellow.

as thou hast given him power over all flesh, that he
should give eternal life to as many as thou hast
given him.

Now it's the will of the Father that every person,
everywhere, be saved. And he inherits life eternal. And
Jesus has the power over all flesh.

But because God put in man a choice to choose for themselves, God will not go against that freedom of choice. Even though he longs for us to be a partaker of his divine inheritance, of his nature itself. But he will not go against our choice. Men will spend a lifetime doing their own thing and going in the way of destruction because God will not overpower man's choice.

You say, but wait a minute. What about Saul on the road to Damascus? What about him? God overpowered him.

God came upon him because God knew that Saul's desire was to please God. But he was an ignorant person concerning life eternal. He said, What I did, I did ignorantly. I wasted the church. I thought I was doing good. I thought this was blasphemy. This preaching of Jesus was blasphemy. This is why I put men and women in prison and consented to others' deaths. I did it ignorantly.

I did it because I was zealous to please God. And God had to just blind him for a few days to let him know, wait a minute, you're ignorant in more ways than one. And I'll just knock you off your high horse and lead you on in blind, that you might see.

But to others, the heart is determined just to be closed, just closed. You see? Pay attention. Verse two,

> as thou hast given him power over all flesh, that he should give eternal life to as many as thou hast given him.

Only when God sees faith and acknowledgement of that faith, like he got Martha to do.

You see how you have to give yourself to him? People come to God in prayer, and they will not acknowledge who he is. We bypass who he is trying to get to God, and God is saying nothing doing.

I have given you the right to come to me boldly only in my son's name. Acknowledge who he is. That's your right-of-way, that's your lifeline.

> *And this is life eternal, that they might know thee the only true God,*

This is life. This is why Jesus came to bring us into that knowledge of who God is.

> *that they might know thee the only true God, and Jesus Christ, whom thou hast sent.*

Whom thou hast sent.

> *I have glorified thee on the earth: I have finished the work which thou gavest me to do.*

And he did. Splendidly, faithfully, obediently. Glory to his name! Wonderful Jesus. Verse 24 of that same chapter,

> *Father, I will that they also, whom thou hast given me, be with me where I am*

This is marvelous.

> *Father, I will that they also,*

Also!

> *whom thou hast given me be with me where I am. That they may behold my glory.*

That they might see who I really am. Hallelujah.

which thou hast given me: for thou lovedst me before the foundation of the world.

This is what he was telling the Jews before Abraham was, I Am. Before Abraham was thought to be born, I Am. And he's standing there praying the Lord's prayer before his father. And before all those that accompanied him. And he's saying, Father, I have glorified your name.

And he said, Father, I will… I want you… This is my desire, to show these that you have given me, the glory that I have with you, even before the foundation of the world. I want them to be blessed to see it. Keep them, give it to them. It's my desire, because they have believed and they love me. And I love them. And you love them with the same love that you love me because they believe on me. Marvelous, isn't it? And not only them, but we're his disciples too, we believe also.

Now the countdown. St. John, I love this. St. John chapter 6. This is leading us up to communion. First, I'll read verses 39 and 40,

And this is the Father's will which hath sent me, that of all which he hath given me I should lose nothing, but should raise it up again at the last day.

And this is the father's will which have sent me. That of all which he hath given me, I should lose nothing, not one. But he lost Judas. He never had Judas… I've chosen 12, and one of you is a devil. And that goes to prove that one cannot be possessed of the devil and of the spirit of Christ at the same time.

And this is the Father's will which hath sent me,
that of all which he hath given me I should lose
nothing, but should raise it up again at the last day.

And this is the will of him that sent me,

Again, the will of him that sent me.

that every one which seeth the Son, and believeth on
him, may have everlasting life: and I will raise him
up at the last day.

You see, this is the authority and the power that Jesus has. That's why it's important to get on the good side of Jesus and get in him. He's the one that's going to do the raising up, you see. Now you try to bypass him to get to God, you're in trouble. Because Jesus is the one who holds the keys. Hallelujah.

Even though it's given over to the church, he has the last say. No preacher anywhere you will stand before in that last day except THE Preacher, at the judgment seat of Christ. And he is the one who's going to say to the angels, take this goat and cast him out in the darkness. And he's going to say to the sheep, enter thou in into the joy of the Lord thy God, putting down some and bringing in others.

So get on the good side. He's the mediator. He's the go-between, you see. His name is your power of attorney to life. Amen. You wonder why we go around saying Jesus. Oh Jesus. It seems like we're never going to get beyond Jesus. Oh Jesus.

But we just love the name. And when we're calling it, many things are rushing through our minds, but we just can't get it said for the power of the name. How many times have we been in conflict, Christians? And we have no time to get out a good prayer. Because the battle is raging. But just to say Jesus. Hell flees.

See, it's the way you say it. And it's how you feel when you say it. And it's what you know when you're saying it that moves heaven and earth. And Jesus says, Father, they call my name, move! Glory be to God!

And God says, Go! Angel Gabriel, go! Michael, go! Soon they're right there to bear us up, right on the scene, that quick. And satan thought he was going to kill us off, going to maim us, blind us, whatever. Put us out in the street with nothing. And we just call one time… JESUS!!

Oh, that prayer means so many words. He said, When you call, I'll say, here I am. He's alive, oh, he's alive. When you get pain wrecking your body, call that name. Say it out loud, Jesus!

What a mighty God we serve. This is why we stand in his presence. Glorifying his name, he compels us to do it. And not only that, we want to do it.

Oh, how many times have I just wanted to be like the apostle Paul? Just… oh Lord, just let me get beside myself. Just let me pretend there's nobody here but you and me. Lord, I just want to stay this way. And the Lord is saying, you gotta move on, there's work to do. Amen.

Many times, being in his presence, I just want to lie down and just stay there for hours, just not move. Just hours in his presence, but obligations call. Glory to God. This is why he says we go in and out and find pasture. Praise his name. All right, get into communion. I'm trying to get there, Lord. It's marvelous.

In your private study, read the entire chapter of St. John 6, all right? But here we're going to go. Before I go to St. John 6, I'm going to turn to St. John 3. I just want you to see something there. Verse 34 through 36, the last three verses, St. John 3,

> *For he whom God hath sent speaketh the words of God: for God giveth not the Spirit by measure unto him.*

Jesus speaking of himself.

> *The Father loveth the Son, and hath given all things into his hand.*

Why? Because he was obedient all the way to death.

> *He that believeth on the Son hath everlasting life:*

Not just in the name, oh, I believe he's a prophet, he's a good man, he was a wise teacher, blah, blah, ah, ah, ah, ah, ah. That's not believing. You're putting him on the same level as man. He's the Son, capital S-O-N, of God.

And he thought it not robbery to be equal with God, Hebrews says.

> *He that believeth on the Son hath everlasting life: and he that believeth not the Son shall not see life; but the wrath of God abideth on him.*

We believe as the scripture says. Back to St. John 6. Verse 47,

> *Verily, verily, I say unto you, He that believeth on me hath everlasting life. I am that bread of life. Your fathers did eat manna in the wilderness, and are*

dead. This is the bread which cometh down from heaven,

which cometh down from heaven

that a man may eat thereof, and not die. I am the living bread which came down from heaven: if any man eat of this bread, he shall live for ever: and the bread that I will give is my flesh, which I will give for the life of the world.

The Jews therefore strove among themselves, saying, How can this man give us his flesh to eat?

They thought he was talking about cannibalism,

Then Jesus said unto them, Verily, verily, I say unto you, Except ye eat the flesh of the Son of man, and drink his blood, ye have no life in you.

Whoso eateth my flesh, and drinketh my blood, hath eternal life; and I will raise him up at the last day.

I tell you, get with Jesus,

For my flesh is meat indeed, and my blood is drink indeed. He that eateth my flesh, and drinketh my blood, dwelleth in me, and I in him. As the living Father hath sent me, and I live by the Father: so he that eateth me, even he shall live by me.

This is that bread which came down from heaven: not as your fathers did eat manna, and are dead: he that eateth of this bread shall live for ever. These things said he in the synagogue, as he taught in Capernaum.

Jesus Christ, the bread, he's not only the breath of life, he's the bread, bread is good. We eat every word like Mary did. She sat at Jesus' feet when Jesus would come through.

We stopped at Bethany, coming out from Jerusalem, and I was in Israel. And there on the scene was a little place, a little spot they said was where Mary and Martha, and Lazarus lived long ago. Another building was erected there, but they said that was the spot.

And even though the crowd was moving on, it was 400 of us. I just stood there, and I said, Lord, how many times did your feet come up this hill to Mary and Martha's house? And how many times did Mary just drop everything she was doing because you were on the scene and you had nothing but life eternal and the golden bits of heaven? And she just chucked everything else away and sat at his feet while Martha was hurrying, trying to make him comfortable.

Good Jewish woman of hospitality, but Mary just said, Oh, he is life itself. I feel so good and so alive when he comes, and the words that flow from his mouth, I've just got to stop and listen. And that she did often. And one day, Martha couldn't take it anymore. She was a dutiful woman.

They say she was a widow. And because she was widowed, Mary and Lazarus had come to live with her. Martha's the one that owned the home, I'm told. History, it's not in my Bible. And they said, Martha wanted to make him comfortable. She wanted him to eat well, she wanted him clean and rested from walking long, dusty trails. She was thinking on the natural and that's good in its place.

But she got upset with Mary because Mary was not helping her get the duties done. And she came and she complained to Jesus. And he said,

> *Martha, Martha, thou art careful and troubled about many things: but one thing is needful: and Mary hath chosen that good part, which shall not be taken away from her.*

Can you see Martha standing there? Just looking at her sister and looking at Christ, and made speechless. And realising, oh, my God, here is life. Here is God. I am so busy going about doing good things. I am missing God!

Can you see her humbling herself at his feet like her sister? To eat the bread that he was feeding. And he said, except you eat the bread, which is my body, and drink my blood, you have no life in you. Martha was not about to go on a diet; she was already lean in spirit. And the Lord was giving her life. How many times has he invited us to come aside, to come apart, to read his word, to let the natural food go and to fast unto him and pray and seek his face? And we say, oh, no, God, not today. I think we've all been guilty.

But he's offering us life. And he said, except we eat him and drink his blood, we can't live. So we have to attend to that which is most important. Put him first. He's not selfish. He's not going to take up our lives, and we don't have time to do the other things. He'll give us ample time. Put him first. Put him first.

Let us stand. Hallelujah. Lord, we praise you.

We give you thanks for you're good. And you are life eternal. This is the will and the reason you sent Jesus, Father. And you have portrayed unto us your reason for sending him. We know the story of his death. We've heard it over and over.

And all the things that have led up to his death. But, Lord, the reason for his dying is portrayed in the book. And you want us to see. You said we must see and believe. We see through the pages and the hearing of the word that Jesus came to give himself a ransom for all mankind.

Without respect to persons, you died for us all. For this cause you came, Lord Jesus. For this cause, you laid down your life in obedience to the will of God the Father. That your Father might be glorified with the sacrificial offering of your body and your blood.

Thank you for coming, thank you for dying in our place. Thank you for taking our place. Thank you, Jesus. Church, thank him. If he means anything to you. Do as he did in bringing Martha to confession in acknowledging that he is the Christ. Say it to him, enter in by faith, believing. Talk to him. Hallelujah. He's desiring to hear our confession of faith. Lord, we believe!

We believe and we know that thou art the Christ. We give you thanks, dear Lord, for your're good. We could not pay the penalty for our sins. We could not pay the debt that was required. Because God required a spotless lamb.

A spotless holy sacrifice. So therefore, we could not, for we were full of sin and guile, Lord God.

But you paid it all. And all to you, Lord Jesus, we owe. We owe you our lives. We owe you thanksgiving and praise continually. Yes, we do. Bless your holy name today.

Oh, Father, God, bring reality to the hearts and minds and the souls of your people. Bring, Lord, life eternal personally to each soul here today. In Jesus' name, Father.

Break every dandable yoke of sin. Loose the bands of wickedness that would hold your people in captivity to your adversary, the devil. Loose the band of wickedness today. Let the oppressed go free. Find up every broken heart.

Wash afresh in the blood today, the blood of Jesus. That was shed for the remission of our sins. We accept this day. You bore all stripes on your back. Thirty-nine, Lord Jesus. Thirty-nine, Lord Jesus. Thirty-nine stripes. Your back was torn. Bleeding, swollen with webs. Cut asunder.

That our bodies and our emotions, our minds, our spirits might be healed. You said by your stripes we are healed. We enter in... We enter in today!

We rebuke sickness. We defy you, oh spirit of infirmity. We defy you in the name of Jesus! You foul spirits that would bring attacks to the hearts. To the muscles. That would bring spasms. That would bring ill disease. In the name of Jesus! My God rebuke you today.

For this cause, Jesus came. That we might have life, and that more abundantly we choose to live. Abundantly so! For the way is made and we enter in by faith in Jesus' name. To our inheritance. Our heavenly inheritance through Christ Jesus our Lord. Father, we commend the healing power of Jesus to flow today.

Destroy all syndromes, Lord. Destroy all sickness, all disease. Destroy today by the power of your word. I speak the word of deliverance. Lord, as we partake. Holy communion today signifying your death, and the reason for your death. As we partake today, Lord, bring a renewal of mind. A remembrance of truth.

Let justice prevail today. Let the power of Jesus Christ penetrate. Move every sin, purify every heart. Jesus, we receive you. Thank you, Father. Thank you for Jesus… Jesus… Take every mind into your captivity. Gather every mind. Every mind, every heart. Do a mighty work by your spirit. Touch every being.

Touch today, touch we ask in your name. Do exceedingly abundantly above what we are able to ask or think, according to your riches in glory, Father. Pour out abundantly upon us today. Do a new thing in us, bring us to higher heights, and deeper depths in Christ Jesus. Bring us into a new awareness, Lord.

Of your holy presence. Bless the Lord, oh my soul. And all that is within me. Bless your holy name. Bless your holy name. Bless your name.

JESUS IS RESURRECTED

First Aired April 3rd, 1994

St. John chapter 20,

> *The first day of the week cometh Mary Magdalene early, when it was yet dark, unto the sepulchre, and seeth the stone taken away from the sepulchre.*

That means Joseph's tomb, sepulchre, is really a tomb. It's not really a grave, it's a tomb.

> *and seeth the stone taken away from the sepulchre. Then she runneth, and cometh to Simon Peter, and to the other disciple, whom Jesus loved,*

meaning John,

> *and saith unto them, They have taken away the Lord out of the sepulchre, and we know not where they have laid him. Peter therefore went forth, and that other disciple, and came to the sepulchre. So they ran both together: and the other disciple did outrun Peter, and came first to the sepulchre. And he stooping down, and looking in, saw the linen clothes lying; yet went he not in.*

He didn't go inside the sepulchre. He just stood at the door of the tomb.

> *Then cometh Simon Peter following him, and went into the sepulchre,*

Isn't that like Peter? Remember when Jesus was walking on the water and all the disciples were in the boat? And Peter said, Lord, if it is really you, bid me come to you. Peter was the only one that got out of the boat! Well, Peter made his way into the tomb. I thank God for Peter. Peter knows how to do things.

Let me read 6 again,

> *Then cometh Simon Peter following him, and went into the sepulchre, and seeth the linen clothes lie, and the napkin, that was about his head, not lying with the linen clothes, but wrapped together in a place by itself.*

Amen.

> *Then went in also that other disciple.*

After he saw Peter, he decided he'd go in too.

> *which came first to the sepulchre, and he saw, and believed.*

He saw and believed.

> *For as yet they knew not the scripture, that he must rise again from the dead.*

Now it wasn't that Jesus didn't tell them. Jesus told them that he was going to rise again. But they refused to hear him. They didn't want to hear that part. Isn't that like us today? Tell me good things, don't tell me the worst.

So when they turned off their ears from hearing about his sufferings and his dying and his death, they didn't hear the other part. You see, so let that teach us a lesson that we hear the good and the bad.

The Word of God said they knew not the scripture, not even at that time.

> *Then the disciples went away again unto their own home. But Mary stood without at the sepulchre weeping: and as she wept, she stooped down, and looked into the sepulchre, and seeth two angels in white sitting,*

Fellas, you got to learn how to hang around. You wonder why there's more women in the church than men? Because we see Jesus. But that doesn't mean that he doesn't want you to see him. You just got to stay a little longer. Amen. Stay a little longer. Mary stood longer and she kept right on weeping. Now Mary was there first. Mary got there a great while before daybreak.

It was morning, but it was still dark. God blessed the name of Mary. It means so much. Help us, Marthas and Jones and Carols and whatever. Help us, Lord. But the Word of God says, verse 11,

> *But Mary stood without at the sepulchre weeping: and as she wept, she stooped down, and looked into the sepulchre, and seeth two angels in white sitting, the one at the head, and the other at the feet, where the body of Jesus had lain. And they say unto her, Woman, why weepest thou?*

Two angels.

> *She saith unto them, Because they have taken away my Lord, and I know not where they have laid him. And when she had thus said, she turned herself back, and saw Jesus standing,*

Jesus had come from hell

and knew not that it was Jesus. Jesus saith unto
her, Woman,

and that using the word woman is a great, endearing word.
A woman means honor. And when they said, when the
angel said woman, and then Jesus said woman, they were
honoring her presence.

Jesus saith unto her, Woman, why weepest thou?
whom seekest thou? She, supposing him to be the
gardener, saith unto him, Sir, if thou have borne him
hence, tell me where thou hast laid him, and I will
take him away.

Oh, what faith. She's gonna take Jesus away. What love.
She's not even thinking about her strength or her weakness.
Just give me Jesus.

Jesus saith unto her, Mary.

No one could call her like that... only Jesus.

She turned herself, and saith unto him, Rabboni;
which is to say, Master. Jesus saith unto her, Touch
me not; for I am not yet ascended to my Father: but
go to my brethren, and say unto them,

See, they didn't stay around long enough for Jesus to tell
them directly. So he had to send Mary the evangelist.

I ascend unto my Father, and your Father;
and to my God, and your God.

Isn't that like Jesus? My Father and your Father. What is
his is ours. Always remember that.

Mary Magdalene came and told the disciples that
she had seen the Lord, and that he had spoken these
things unto her.

Then the same day at evening, being the first day of
the week, when the doors were shut where the
disciples were assembled for fear of the Jews, came
Jesus and stood in the midst, and saith unto
them, Peace be unto you.

Speaking of himself. See the capital P. He's speaking of
himself, Peace.

And when he had so said, he shewed unto
them his hands and his side. Then were the disciples
glad, when they saw the Lord. Then said Jesus to
them again, Peace be unto you: as my Father hath
sent me, even so send I you. And when he had said
this, he breathed on them, and saith unto
them, Receive ye the Holy Ghost: whose soever sins
ye remit, they are remitted unto them; and whose
soever sins ye retain, they are retained.

But Thomas, one of the twelve, called Didymus, was
not with them when Jesus came. The other disciples
therefore said unto him, We have seen the Lord. But
he said unto them, Except I shall see in his hands
the print of the nails, and put my finger into the
print of the nails, and thrust my hand into his side, I
will not believe. And after eight days,

Because of unbelief, he had to wait that long. But can you
imagine what was going on in his mind? All the other
disciples were excited about the appearance of Jesus and
Didymus, Thomas, whom we called Doubting Thomas; he

couldn't stand it because he thought they were hallucinating. But really, he did not believe them.

And that's where the spirit of hallucination comes, into the being of unbelief. It's bad to have unbelief because it brings all kinds of ungodly thoughts. It's terrible not to believe the report that's given of Jesus Christ.

Because if we don't have faith, then we are going to receive negative faith. And that's every diabolical lie the devil can tell. Every man has faith, but either it's positive or it's negative. Either we believe God or we believe the devil. Thomas chose not to believe. So that made him think that the others were being deluded. What a lie, what a lie.

People think that today, they think that of us today. They think that we celebrate the resurrection of Jesus Christ because we want a crutch to lean on. Not a crutch, he's a rod, amen, Jesus.

> *And after eight days again his disciples were within, and Thomas with them: then came Jesus, the doors being shut,*

He's in his glorified body now…

> *and stood in the midst, and said, Peace be unto you. Then saith he to Thomas,*

 No one told him because he heard him. He's spirit now, and he heard him.

> *Then saith he to Thomas, Reach hither thy finger, and behold my hands; and reach hither thy hand, and thrust it into my side: and be not faithless, but believing.*

132

But why wouldn't he let Mary Magdalene touch him? It's simply because he said, I have not ascended to my father yet.

So between the time that he showed himself to Mary Magdalene and would not allow her to touch him and the time that he appeared to his disciples and let Thomas see his hands and thrust his hand into his side, he had been home to the Father. God the Father had glorified his body. It's amazing.

He has no respect of persons. He said, and he doesn't lie. So he says in verse 17,

> *touch me not for I am not yet ascended to my father, but go to my brethren and say unto them, I ascend unto my father.*

See, you see it? See what he said? I'm going, I'm going to my father first, but I'll see you. I'm coming to you and say unto them, I ascend unto my father and your father and to my God and your God. So Mary went and told them what he said.

And then later on that evening, same day, Jesus comes to his disciples, but Thomas wasn't there because Thomas didn't believe anyhow. Thomas thought… he's dead and he's gone, that's it!

I'm wondering if Thomas was part of the Sadducees before he followed Jesus. But the point is eight days later, a whole week and a day later, Jesus says, Come Thomas, thrust your hand in my side and be not faithless, but believing. Because he had already ascended to his father, he had to go and do his reporting and be glorified, his glorified body like we shall have.

See, he's the first fruit of the resurrection. Now the saints got up and walked. So they were resurrected, too, remember? But Jesus ascended to the Father and our Father, to his God and our God, but he came back that evening and fellowship with his brethren, glorious Jesus.

And that's why he wanted Mary to take the news to them that he was risen. But watch Thomas. Verse 27,

> *Then saith he to Thomas, Reach hither thy finger, and behold my hands; and reach hither thy hand, and thrust it into my side: and be not faithless, but believing. And Thomas answered and said unto him, My Lord and my God. Jesus saith unto him, Thomas, because thou hast seen me, thou hast believed: blessed are they that have not seen, and yet have believed.*

Now remember when John bent down and went into the tomb, and he saw the way the napkin that was on Jesus's head was laid, how it was folded and laid. And he said, I believe, I believe, I believe. But yet he had not seen him.

But just to see the evidence of what covered him, laid there. You know why? Because he was familiar with Jesus Christ. He stayed close to him, that disciple whom he loved.

So he knew how Jesus did things. You know, when a loved one passed away, then we become, you know, we, we come into recollection of what they did and how they did things, how they handled their hands, how they sat and ate and how they took off their shoes or how they wore their clothing. And it means so much to you.

And it seems like you… You look for that in somebody else. And it reminds you so much of that dear departed one. And so when John saw the way the napkin was laid, he said, I believe. We just read it. I believe. That was it. That's all he knew; he couldn't go any further.

> *Thomas answered and said unto him, My Lord and my God. Jesus saith unto him, Thomas, because thou hast seen me, thou hast believed: blessed are they that have not seen, and yet have believed.*

> *And many other signs truly did Jesus in the presence of his disciples, which are not written in this book: but these are written, that ye might believe that Jesus is the Christ,*

that we might believe

> *that Jesus is the Christ, the Son of God; and that believing ye might have life through his name.*

> *After these things Jesus shewed himself again to the disciples at the sea of Tiberias; and on this wise shewed he himself. There were together Simon Peter, and Thomas called Didymus, and Nathanael of Cana in Galilee, and the sons of Zebedee, and two other of his disciples. Simon Peter saith unto them, I go a fishing. They say unto him, We also go with thee. They went forth, and entered into a ship immediately; and that night they caught nothing.*

> *But when the morning was now come, Jesus stood on the shore: but the disciples knew not that it was Jesus.*

> *Then Jesus saith unto them, Children, have ye any meat?*

Because they're acting like children. When he rose, he said, Go and tell my brethren.

> *They answered him, No. And he said unto them, Cast the net on the right side of the ship, and ye shall find. They cast therefore, and now they were not able to draw it for the multitude of fishes. Therefore that disciple whom Jesus loved saith unto Peter, It is the Lord. Now when Simon Peter heard that it was the Lord, he girt his fisher's coat unto him, (for he was naked,) and did cast himself into the sea.*

He was stripped. That means he had no clothes on. Jesus saw him before he put the fisher's coat around him. But to give reverence to the presence of the Lord. Isn't that like us today? The Lord is always around us. He's always looking at us. What the Lord is striving to do is to awake them unto him, unto life, unto the spirit of God. That they might walk in the spirit.

See, when they went fishing, they thought maybe Jesus had gone back to heaven to his God and his Father. But Jesus was still around. In his glorified body. And he's still around. Verse 8,

> *And the other disciples came in a little ship; (for they were not far from land, but as it were two hundred cubits,) dragging the net with fishes.*

> *As soon then as they were come to land, they saw a fire of coals there, and fish laid thereon, and bread.*

136

Jesus cooking,

> *Jesus saith unto them, Bring of the fish which ye have now caught.*
>
> *Simon Peter went up, and drew the net to land full of great fishes, an hundred and fifty and three: and for all there were so many, yet was not the net broken. Jesus saith unto them, Come and dine.*

Now just watch their behavior, it's very interesting.

> *And none of the disciples durst ask him, Who art thou? knowing that it was the Lord. Jesus then cometh, and taketh bread, and giveth them, and fish likewise. This is now the third time that Jesus shewed himself to his disciples, after that he was risen from the dead.*
>
> *So when they had dined, Jesus saith to Simon Peter, Simon, son of Jonas, lovest thou me more than these?*

Watch Peter.

> *He saith unto him, Yea, Lord; thou knowest that I love thee. He saith unto him, Feed my lambs. He saith to him again the second time, Simon, son of Jonas, lovest thou me? He saith unto him, Yea, Lord; thou knowest that I love thee. He saith unto him, Feed my sheep.*
>
> *He saith unto him the third time, Simon, son of Jonas, lovest thou me? Peter was grieved because he said unto him the third time, Lovest thou me? And he said unto him, Lord, thou knowest all things;*

thou knowest that I love thee. Jesus saith unto
him, Feed my sheep.

Verily, verily, I say unto thee, When thou wast
young, thou girdedst thyself, and walkedst whither
thou wouldest: but when thou shalt be old, thou
shalt stretch forth thy hands, and another shall gird
thee, and carry thee whither thou wouldest not. This
spake he, signifying by what death he should glorify
God.

The Lord Jesus is giving Peter to know that he's going to
die for his sake, that he will become a martyr.

And when he had spoken this, he saith unto
him, Follow me.

Up until then, Peter was going fishing, and Peter was doing
this and that, but Jesus said, Follow me.

Then Peter, turning about, seeth the disciple whom
Jesus loved following; which also leaned on his
breast at supper, and said, Lord, which is he that
betrayeth thee? Peter seeing him saith to Jesus,
Lord, and what shall this man do? Jesus saith unto
him, If I will that he tarry till I come, what is that to
thee? follow thou me.

Then went this saying abroad among the brethren,
that that disciple should not die: yet Jesus said not
unto him, He shall not die; but, If I will that he tarry
till I come, what is that to thee?

And John did tarry, all the way out to the isle of Patmos.
Peter was already home in glory. By the way of death, they
crucified Peter. They also crucified Peter. Peter was long

gone, and John was still on earth, getting persecuted severely.

That's how we have the book of Revelation. So don't ever shy away from persecution, amen, and trouble and woe. God is only getting you in readiness for greater things, greater things! So don't have a pity party. And if you do, encourage yourself in the Lord and get up and go.

Verse 24,

> *This is the disciple which testifieth of these things, and wrote these things: and we know that his testimony is true.*
>
> *And there are also many other things which Jesus did, the which, if they should be written every one, I suppose that even the world itself could not contain the books that should be written. Amen.*

And I'm telling you the world is still writing. We are yet in this world, and we're still writing about Jesus. The things that he's yet doing by his spirit. Praise God. So this is the true story of the resurrection of Jesus Christ and some of his deeds that he did after he rose from the grave. Amen.

1st Corinthians chapter 15. Hallelujah. Now, Paul was not saved at that time; he was still Saul. He learned as a wise and apt Pharisee, a rabbi… Paul was a rabbi. He learned from the scriptures, being yet dark, wise to what was written, but not wise enough to see through the veil that had already been ripped and torn apart in the temple when Jesus died.

Paul, yet under the law of Moses is what I'm really saying.

He sincerely thought that Jesus Christ was an impostor, like so many today do. He did it ignorantly, which means he did not know the truth like the others did.

And so being zealous for the things of God Almighty under the law of Moses, he persecuted the church of the Lord Jesus Christ. He consented to some's death, and he also consented to some imprisonment. The Christians because he hated the gospel that they preached.

He thought it was a lie to carry the people away from the true and living God, not realizing that it was God in the Son. So he ignorantly persecuted the body of Jesus Christ. Amen.

1 Corinthians chapter 15 explains it more thoroughly,

> *Moreover, brethren, I declare unto you the gospel which I preached unto you, which also ye have received, and wherein ye stand; by which also ye are saved,*

The gospel, we're saved by the gospel of Jesus Christ, whom Paul preached. Aren't we? Whom St. John preached and Luke, the physician, wrote about, Mathew and brother Mark. That's why we're saved today…those jews, those good old jews! Amen. Oh, there's some bad ones, and I'm sure you know about them.

These happen to be the good ones, giving us a good report. And how many believe their report today? Do you believe that Jesus is God the Son? And that He came for you, that He died for you? That He went to Hell on your behalf? Amen, that you wouldn't have to be locked and bound there. Glory be to God, do you believe that Jesus is risen again from the dead?

Do you believe that Jesus Christ has ascended onto the Father? To the throne of the Most High God? Do you believe that he is there right now, sitting at the right hand of the Father interceding for you right now? Do you believe that He is praying for you right now?

Glory to God! Hallelujah! He says, verse 3

> *For I delivered unto you first of all that which I also received,*

See, before we can deliver the Word of God, we must first receive it.

> *how that Christ died for our sins according to the scriptures;*

That's why we have the scriptures to read and believe

> *and that he was buried, and that he rose again the third day according to the scriptures:*

Hallelujah,

> *and that he was seen of Cephas, then of the twelve: after that, he was seen of above five hundred brethren at once; of whom the greater part remain unto this present, but some are fallen asleep.*

In other words, when Paul was writing this, some of the Saints, some of the 500 brethren were still alive, glory to God, Hallelujah, he said, but some have fallen asleep. Some had already gone to their grave. Verse 7,

> *After that, he was seen of James; then of all the apostles.*

Now, how did he know all of this? Glory to God, verse 8,

And last of all he was seen of me also, as of one born out of due time.

Due time, precious hearts, Praise God last of all he was seen of me, and we can say wait a minute, brother Paul, last of all he was seen of me. Can't we say that? Glory to God, verse 9,

For I am the least of the apostles, that am not meet to be called an apostle, because I persecuted the church of God.

Even though he is an Apostle, he says He's not worthy to carry that title because he persecuted the Church of God. Maybe he thinks at this point that he's not worthy, but God made him worthy, God chose Him to be an Apostle. Even while he was persecuted in the church, God had already foreordained Paul to be an Apostle of the gospel of Jesus Christ, Amen. Let me read verse 9 again,

For I am the least of the apostles, that am not meet to be called an apostle, because I persecuted the church of God. But by the grace of God I am what I am:

And we all can say that it's by the grace of God.

And his grace which was bestowed upon me was not in vain; but I laboured more abundantly than they all:

In other words. He was making up for lost time. Glory to God.

Yet not I, but the grace of God which was with me. Therefore whether it were I or they, so we preach, and ye believed.

*Now if Christ be preached that he rose from the
dead, how say some among you that there is no
resurrection of the dead?*

As the Sadducees, you see? The sect of the Sadducees
believed God, but they didn't believe in the resurrection of
the dead, and this is why the Apostle is writing this. He
says,

*Now if Christ be preached that he rose from the
dead, how say some among you that there is no
resurrection of the dead? But if there be no
resurrection of the dead, then is Christ not
risen: and if Christ be not risen, then is our
preaching vain, and your faith is also vain.*

Yea, and we are found false witnesses of God;

That is if Christ be not risen…

*because we have testified of God that he raised up
Christ: whom he raised not up, if so be that the
dead rise not. For if the dead rise not, then is not
Christ raised: and if Christ be not raised, your
faith is vain; ye are yet in your sins.*

That's why we better believe, Glory to God!

*Then they also which are fallen asleep in Christ are
perished.*

In other words, there's no hope for them, amen.

*If in this life only we have hope in Christ, we are of
all men most miserable.*

Have you seen people who have no hope? In this life
whatsoever?

I don't mean of even Christ at this point, but they just have no hope for life. They have no hope to live, no desire to live. They are oppressed so much that even the desire to live and to move and have their being, to function... that hope is all gone, and you have yourself a vegetable that's only existing. There are a lot of people in this world like this today. And this is what the Apostle Paul is saying. We're of all men, most miserable if we do not have this hope, if we do not believe that Jesus is raised from the dead.

This is why I ask you how many of you believe? He says verse 20,

> But now is Christ risen from the dead, and become the firstfruits of them that slept. For since by man came death,

by Adam that is.

> by man came also the resurrection of the dead.

Jesus Christ, the second man Adam,

> For as in Adam all die, even so in Christ shall all be made alive.

Do you believe this! Say amen, church! Glory to God! Sometimes I wonder, I honestly wonder Lord... Glory to God! But if you're alive, you should be rejoicing, saying amen to the word! Glory hallelujah! But he says, verse 23,

> But every man in his own order: Christ the firstfruits; afterward they that are Christ's at his coming. Then cometh the end, when he shall have delivered up the kingdom to God,

When he had he shall have delivered up the kingdom of God to God.

> *even the Father; when he shall have put down all rule and all authority and power*

You see, Jesus is now ruling by all authority, all power, and he's ruling over all. I don't care how you think you might be your own person, He's still Lord. He's Lord in Heaven, and he's Lord over the Earth. That right is his because he is risen, glory to God! And the Word of God says, verse 25,

> *For he must reign, till he hath put all enemies under his feet.*

Jesus Christ is going to rule until every enemy is put down under his feet! Hallelujah! See, we're not celebrating somebody who rose from the dead for our sins. We're celebrating the greatest warrior that ever existed!

He's a fighter, we're serving a God of battles! He's a warmonger! You ever seen people... just love the fight, no matter what, they just love the fight, always getting into problems and trouble. Look at Jesus, amen, he goes on the offensive.

Remember what God said to satan one day? Has thou considered my servant Job? That there's none like him in all the earth. A righteous man and one that fears God? He started a fight! Glory be to God in the highest! When Jesus went to that cross, he started a fight like never before. satan thought he had him, but Jesus said no. I'm coming on your turf, and I'm gonna beat you up and I'm gonna take the keys. But I'm not going to just do you in just yet, I have work to do on the earth yet. Amen.

I gotta encourage my brethren, Jesus, looking up from hell, and he sees his poor brethren shut behind the door for fear of the Jews that have consented to Jesus being crucified. So Jesus said I have to go and encourage my brethren, but in the meantime, the war is on down here.

You go ahead, you fear, and you tremble, but I want my keys. See, satan is a thief. When he was cast out of Heaven, he was cast out as a thief, not only in pride, but he was the biggest thief; he stole the keys. Do you know that? He stole the keys of death, hell, and the grave.

And God said, 'That's all right, let him have them. The moment that he thinks not, take them!' And Jesus took them! That's why the Christian does not fear death. And we don't fear, allowing our body to be put in the ground. Praise God, and we know that satan has no dominion over us. Because he has no dominion over Christ, and we are Christ's.

Hallelujah, we belong to Jesus Christ in this present world! And we know the victory, and this is why we go around starting fights. This is why we visit the hospitals: we come to beat satan up. The affliction that he puts on people… we say, 'Take your hands off! Take your filth back!' Amen, that's what we go to do.

We go to encourage the sick, but in the meantime, we're putting up a fight! Spirit against spirit! The spirit of man against the spirit of the devil! 'Get your filthy hands off the property of God!' That person could be the biggest sinner who ever lived. I know about it, I visited one. What a fight over that man's soul… and God says Don't give up on him.

He was the biggest gambler, they tell me around here, and the Lord said, 'Go bring him unto me.' I walked into the

146

hospital, and this man was laying up there, huge, long, and tall. I didn't know the man was in a coma. I went to visit a friend of mine, pleading to God, 'Please don't take her Lord, she's the only friend I've got in Montclair.'

Nine o'clock a.m. I took my son to school, and I headed to the hospital, walked into the hospital room, the Lord had breathed again upon her; she was living. And this man's wife was visiting her early that morning, and she introduced me to her. And she said her husband is here in the hospital and he's in intensive care with heart failure. I said,

> "Oh, Ma'am, do you mind if I go and pray with him?"

She said,

> "Oh no…"

Neither one of them told me what a booger of a man he was. So, I marched all around and down the hall until I got to the coronary unit. I told the nurse at the station who I wanted to see, and she pointed over there. And I went up to his bed and I called him by his name. I learned his name from his wife, and I touched him, and he said,

> "Hmm!"

And I said

> "Mr. I just met your wife here in the hospital moments ago, and she gave me permission to come and pray with you."

And he said,

"Get your hands off me!"

I said,

"All right."

I didn't know the Lord had brought the man out of a coma. I touched him, and God touched him! Brought him right out of the coma, but I didn't learn this until I got back to the room of my friend. And I stood there, my hands down. I'm trying to reverence him, and I stood there, you know, I'm praying, and I said,

"I will be back."

I marched on, he cut his eye around at me, and I marched on. I went back and I told his wife. And I didn't know why they were looking like this when I walked in. I said,

"He let me pray with him, but he didn't want me to touch him."

They said,

"What did he say?"

And I said,

"He told me to get my hands off him."

They said,

"He talked?'

And I said,

"Yes, he wasn't really too nice, but I prayed for him."

They said,

"He was in a coma!"

I said,

"A coma?"

She said,

"Yes, I've been here all night. The hospital called me and they told me that he was leaving and that I should get here."

And she said,

"Ma'am, he's been in a coma all night. When I left the room, he was in a coma."

I said

"Not now."

She said

"Let me go!"

And she went down, and I was still in the room when she came back. She said to my friend,

"It's true, he's awake!"

But see, Jesus Christ is the resurrection and the life! And for days, the kingdom of darkness and the kingdom of light wrestled over that man's soul. And one day the Lord told me to go. In the meantime, they moved him out of intensive care, they had to take off, amputate one of his legs, and I walked in that particular room and he said,

"You can pray for me, but don't you come near me!"

"I'm tired of you, mister. I've tried to honor you ever since I met you, but you don't order me around. I'm here because God sent me." I said.

See all before I was humble, but it was time to put on my battle garments. And my battle garment is my mouth.

I said,

"Don't you tell me what not to do?"

I said,

"Ma'am…"

I'm talking to his wife. I said,

"Do you believe God? Do you believe in the power of God?

She said,

"Yes, I do."

I said,

"All right, join with me, we're bringing this devil down!"

And we stood there at the table looking at him, praying,

"You foul devil, you coming out of him!"

And I bound satan up and I cast him out of him and I said,

"I don't want any more lip from you!"

And I said,

"And furthermore. I'm not coming back here unless God sends me, now you think about that!"

And I walked out on my heels. The next day, I got a phone call from the hospital,

> "He's dying. He's really leaving this time. Can you come?" they said.

I said,

> "Not unless God sends me, I'm not coming."

And I walked on to my car, and I went on and got my daughter some sneakers she needed for gym. But as I drove, I started praying,

> "Lord, I don't want to harden my heart against him because that is a soul slipping out into eternity, and he hasn't met you yet. Now, if it's your will that I go, I'll go, but if you don't tell me, Lord, I'm not going."

And the Lord didn't tell me, and I kept right on driving to the mall. Well, the following day I got another call saying,

> "He's just barely here."

The Lord said,

> *"Go."*

And I went, but I went armed with the Word of God. I turned to the scripture in St. John where it says,

> *where the worm dieth not and the fire is not quenched.*

And I got right over him, and I said,

> "Keep your mouth shut, I know you're awake. You can keep your eyes closed all you want."

I said,

>"But God sent me, and I'm telling you what God says. If you don't stop your stubbornness and accept Jesus Christ as your personal Savior, you're going where the fire is not quenched! You filthy old worm, is that what you want?"

>"Mmmm." He said.

I got right over him again.

>"Let me read this to you, don't you move," I said.

And the Lord said,

>*"Put your hand on his chest and rebuke the devil."*

So I laid my hands and he started,

>"HMMM!"

His arms all full of tubes, and he's mumbling, and I said,

>"Don't you open your mouth! I dare you to open your mouth, you hold your peace, and you listen. I'm striving to win your soul, you stupid man!"

And so, I mean... I really had to get rough like that to this man. I've never in my life won a soul like that. And so I read the scriptures to him, and at this point, that man started yelling! He yelled at the top of his voice, he screamed! But see, it was the devils, the devils were tormented inside of him. They meant to take that man out of here! And the nurse from the nursing station, which was right there outside of the door, came running in, she said,

>"What's wrong? What's happening to him?"

And I stood there like a soldier, and the wife said,

"He needs a shot; he's in pain."

It was a lie; he didn't need a shot, he was in pain all right! The pains of hell! Glory be to God! And the Lord sent me to snatch that man's soul from hell itself! And the Lord was telling him through the word, If you do not repent, you're going to hell where the worm dieth not and the fire is not quenched.

In other words, you… You foul worm, you're going to hell. And the fire is not going to die down for you; the fire is not quenched. So the nurse gave him a needle. We were outside the door. I looked at his wife, and she looked at me, and I tell you, I thought I'd burst. I said,

"I'm not finished. I'm going back in again."

She said,

"You going back?"

I said,

"I'm going back in, I've got to do what God sent me to do." I said, "Sister, what you're really looking at is a demonic war here. I'm going to win. The Lord sent me to win. I don't like losing."

So we went back in and we got up even before the nurse walked out. We came back in and the nurse gave us, and especially me, a dirty look because she knew, she was right outside the hall, she gave us a dirty look. And I said to his wife, I said,

"Sister, God has to take him, because this man is grossly wicked." I said, "Do you understand what

I'm saying?" I said, "He's going to make it, the moment that he calls on the name of the Lord... he's going out of here, God's gonna snatch him out immediately."

She said,

"All right."

I said,

"Do you understand?"

She says

"I understand."

I went back over and I finished my work, and I said,

"Mr... I'm leaving you in the hands of God now. The battle is won, but you've got to call upon his name. Make sure you do."

And I left at the end of the week. They're calling me. I think it was that Thursday or that Friday morning, my friend said,

"He's gone," and she said, "Mrs. Davis, a funny thing happened. His wife told me that the nurse..."

At that point, the wife was hospitalized also, and she was there when her husband died, but she was in another room on the same floor.

She said,

"He called... said the nurse walked in and said he opened his eyes, looked up to the ceiling and said

154

'Jesus have mercy' and he expired just as the Lord prophesied unto him and unto his wife."

I only mentioned that to let you know what a fight it is sometimes over souls. That satan is determined, and their heart is so determined not to yield to God. But God is our life, He is our resurrection, He is our quickening spirit. And God quickened that man's spirit by His spirit and brought him life, even though the body died, amen.

He's home with Jesus. And when I get home, I'm gonna look him up, I'm gonna confess to him that in my lifetime, I've never fought a fight like that. And had it not been for the love of God, I would have long given up on him. But God is love and long-suffering. Praise God, not willing that any man perish. He's long-suffering…

Okay, back to First Corinthians 15. We're looking at Christ reigning or ruling until his enemies become his footstool, Verse 26,

> *The last enemy that shall be destroyed is death.*

That means altogether, he's got his keys, but he's going to be destroyed.

> *For he hath put all things under his feet. But when he saith all things are put under him, it is manifest that he is excepted, which did put all things under him. And when all things shall be subdued unto him, then shall the Son also himself be subject unto him*

Meaning God the Father,

> *That put all things under him, that God may be all in all. Else what shall they do which are baptized for the dead, if the dead rise not at all? why are they*

155

then baptized for the dead? And why stand we in
jeopardy every hour? I protest by your rejoicing
which I have in Christ Jesus our Lord, I die daily.

In other words, to those things that are displeasing to God,
He says I die daily. When God enlightens me to that thing
that is going to destroy my life, I die to it. That's the growth
of a Christian; we don't remain stunted. Once we accept
Christ as our personal Savior, we grow, and the more He
enlightens us to those things that would destroy us or that
would bring us life to our souls, Paul says I die daily. I die
to it, Amen.

Now he's speaking in verse 32

If after the manner of men I have fought with beasts
at Ephesus, what advantageth it me, if the dead rise
not? let us eat and drink; for to morrow we die. Be
not deceived: evil communications corrupt good
manners

Don't kid yourself, is what we would say today. Hang
around evil, it's gonna make you evil. He says,

Awake to righteousness, and sin not; for some have
not the knowledge of God:

And the knowledge of God is that he is able to keep us
from sin. You don't hear this preached today, but it's still the
truth, He said sin not.

for some have not the knowledge of God: I
speak this to your shame.

We've got no business being ignorant of this fact, that God
is able to keep us IF we choose to be kept. He says,

> *But some man will say, How are the dead raised up? and with what body do they come? Thou fool, that which thou sowest is not quickened, except it die:*

See, when we die to this the cares of this world and to the lust of the pleasures of this life, that's when we are made alive unto God, and that's why Paul says 'thou fool'. In other words, can't you understand this? Except you die, you cannot be quickened. That's what he's really saying.

Verse 37,

> *and that which thou sowest, thou sowest not that body that shall be, but bare grain, it may chance of wheat, or of some other grain: but God giveth it a body as it hath pleased him, and to every seed his own body.*

Now I'm gonna jump down in verse 42,

> *So also is the resurrection of the dead. It is sown in corruption; it is raised in incorruption: it is sown in dishonour; it is raised in glory: it is sown in weakness; it is raised in power:*

Hallelujah. Now, if you listen to some songs and you listen to some preachers and you listen to some prayers, it's never with victory. It's still corrupted, it is still dishonorable, and it's still weak, and that's not why Jesus came. Jesus came that we might be triumphant. That's why he told Mary to go and tell the brethren, 'I Ascend to your my God and your God to my Father and your Father.' Amen, as I am, so are you, is what Jesus is saying? What is mine is yours? That's what Jesus is saying. And he is saying it today. It's on record. It still stands, Glory to God. So he says, verse 44,

It is sown a natural body; it is raised a spiritual
body. There is a natural body, and there is a
spiritual body. And so it is written, The first man
Adam was made a living soul; the last Adam was
made a quickening spirit.

So we have a soul, and God quickens our spirit by His
Spirit, Amen, Hallelujah!

Howbeit that was not first which is spiritual, but
that which is natural;

In other words, Adam was made a natural body, you see,

and afterward that which is spiritual. The first
man is of the earth, earthy: the second man is the
Lord from heaven.

Glory, Hallelujah,

As is the earthy, such are they also that are earthy:
and as is the heavenly, such are they also that are
heavenly. And as we have borne the image of the
earthy, we shall also bear the image of the
heavenly.

In other words, we shall have a glorified body as Jesus has.
He had to break it down to the Corinthians in this manner
so they could fully understand what he was saying.

If we were to say to people, Praise God, I shall have a
glorified body! Amen, and leave it at that; many would not
understand. Only those who are with Christ or have been
with Christ. But those who are just listening, or maybe have
come to the Lord, but don't understand spiritual language
yet, it has to be broken down to them. Or to the babes in
Christ, you see?

So this is what Paul is doing: he's breaking it down to each and every person, what it truly means to have a glorified body. And this is why he goes all the way back to Adam, do you understand?

Ok verse 50,

> *Now this I say, brethren, that flesh and blood cannot*
> *inherit the kingdom of God;*

Such as we, you see? Such is your physical body, the body that you live in, is your house, or your earthly tabernacle.

> *flesh and blood cannot inherit the kingdom of God;*
> *neither doth corruption inherit*
> *incorruption. Behold, I shew you a mystery; We*
> *shall not all sleep, but we shall all be changed,*

Everybody's not going by the way of death. Amen. Many will die, but not everybody. Praise God, but all will be changed. In the air, those that are dead are gonna be raised before those who remain. Can't you just look, just imagine that now. Think about it, think on it, and see that change. You know, like an artist sees glorious things and they put it on canvas or paper. All right, be that artist today.

Look at those folks by the word of power being resurrected from the dead, coming up out of their graves and changing right before your eyes, and you too. Glory be to God, we that remain, and I really believe that Jesus is coming in our day. I believe it because so much is fulfilling so rapidly.

I believe it. Glory be to God that this is the generation that Jesus was talking about, according to the scriptures, that will remain at his coming. Hallelujah.

And our eyes are going to behold God bringing the, by the power of God, bringing those that have died in Christ Jesus up out of their graves. Hallelujah. And shake off the old grave clothes. Praise God and all the dust and the decay, glory to God. Hallelujah. Amen.

And we that remain, praise God, are gonna change, amen, from the flesh and the blood of this corruptible body. And in the air, we're gonna put on our new glorified body and be ushered in the twinkling of an eye into the presence of the Most High God. Hallelujah.

Talking about space, outer space, glory to God, out of here, through space, at home. What a mighty God we serve. My God, that's the hope of every Christian today. And if that's not your hope, you are most miserable. I do agree with Brother Paul. Praise God.

This is our whole reason for living. This is our reason for going through the trials that we go through. This is why we go through humbly like we are. Amen. In Jesus' name. This is why we take the things we take. If we didn't have this hope, praise God, we'd be out there fighting just like you in the natural. Hallelujah. But our hope is eternal!

God is going to fulfill our hope. Talking about a day of rejoicing. Remember what Jesus said? He said, they shall laugh and you shall weep now, but later you shall rejoice and they shall mourn.

Well, honey, they're going to mourn. Glory be to God when they see us go. Hallelujah. In the great tribulation of the world, like never before, the sufferings like humanity has never known shall immediately fall upon this world. Glory to God in the highest. Precious ones, come out from the world.

Do not receive the work of the devil. Do not receive the mark of the beast. If you lust after the riches and cares of this life, forsake them. Amen. The greatest riches that you will ever have is Christ Jesus and the inherited kingdom of God. Amen! Through Christ Jesus. He is our inheritance, and all that Jesus has is ours. Glory to God!

Everything that he owns is ours. Just be patient. It's not long! Glory be to God. We're getting out of here with our glorified bodies. Praise God!

Don't let the subtlety of the devil take you away from the love of God. Come on in. Get in fully. Hallelujah. Don't be afraid of death. Death has no sting. Death can't own you. Hallelujah, Jesus. You see, everybody will not sleep, meaning death cannot put people to death.

God only uses it. God only uses it to put us to sleep. Glory to God. He calls us from our earthly bodies because it's corrupt. The body gives out on us. Amen.

Hallelujah. Daily, we die to the body or in the body. We're dying. Amen. But our life lives on. Praise God. We live. We're alive. Amen. Those that God has called out of the body, if they died in Christ, amen, they are alive just as you are, but they're just on the other side. That's what death is. Amen. Glory be to God.

Now that other death, amen, those that die outside of Christ, now that's a different story. This is why we, like Paul, persuade men everywhere to repent and receive Jesus Christ, who is the resurrection and the life.

Amen. Jesus is the one who resurrects us from death, so don't fear. Put your hope, put your life, put your trust in Jesus Christ. He's conquered death, hell, and the grave. Nothing can hold you down. Glory, hallelujah.

Praise our God. Look at verse 51 again, and I'm going all the way through.

> *Behold, I shew you a mystery; We shall not all sleep, but we shall all be changed, in a moment, in the twinkling of an eye,*

That's how fast it is, precious ones. That's how quick God is.

> *at the last trump: for the trumpet shall sound, and the dead shall be raised incorruptible, and we shall be changed.*

It shall be. Glory, Hallelujah!

> *For this corruptible must put on incorruption, and this mortal must put on immortality.*

Where we shall live forever.

> *So when this corruptible shall have put on incorruption, and this mortal shall have put on immortality, then shall be brought to pass the saying that is written, Death is swallowed up in victory.*

Hallelujah. Victory… shall overpower death. Victory, the spirit of victory, shall overpower death! Hallelujah! Glory to God. Oh, wonderful Savior. He is our life, and bless God we by faith we have the victory now.

We claim the victory now. We rejoice for the victory. Praise God, that is in Christ Jesus, and we are in Christ Jesus. So we have victory. Holy Jesus. Holy Jesus.

And then he says to old death.

> *O death, where is thy sting? O grave, where is thy victory?*

Couldn't hold Jesus down, because there was no sin in him. Couldn't hold Jesus down, because he was too full of life, too full of the power of God. Praise God, he won't be able to hold us down, because sin will not have dominion over us either. That's our determination as a born-again child of God.

That's why Jesus said you must be born again by the Spirit of God. Amen. The Spirit of God is from heaven. See, Jesus came from heaven. I just read to you that Adam came from the earth. Jesus came from heaven, and that's why satan could not win over him. And we are of heaven, because we are in heavenly places with Jesus, so he can't win over us either.

That's what Jesus has wrought for us. This is why we preach Jesus morning, noon, and night, and through the night, through all the night, if possible. We preach Jesus because this is what he means to us. He says, verse 56,

> *The sting of death is sin;*

If death has power over you, it's because of sin.

> *The sting of death is sin; and the strength of sin is the law. But thanks be to God, which giveth us the victory through our Lord Jesus Christ.*

You see, we have the victory. He giveth us, present tense, he gives us the victory continually, continually, throughout our life, continually. The life that is in Christ Jesus is our victory.

Through our Lord Jesus Christ.

> *Therefore, my beloved brethren, be ye stedfast, unmoveable, always abounding in the work of the Lord,*

Just keep on working. Amen. Precious ones, you that have been recipients of others in here, that have come after your soul, it is because of the commandment right here. Amen. To come after you, and persuade you to come unto Jesus, and be made whole. Praise God. It's the love of God. It's not just the servant of the Lord only. Yes, the servant of the Lord that's coming and persuading you, but it's not just that individual.

It's God in them, coming after you, and saying, Be made whole. I am your lover. I am your soul's love. Be made whole. Praise God in the highest. I have better things for you than what you are abiding in. Glory be to God. I give unto you life, where there's no corruption, and no guile, no decay. I give unto you the beauty of my kingdom.

Praise God in the highest. It's yours, I give it to you. I have room enough for you and many more. That's what he's saying. Come, my beloved. That's what he is saying today. It's a love story. It's a victory, it's triumphant victory, victorious story, and it's true. It's not a fairy tale like we sit down and read to our children, and our grands, and whatever. This story is true.

My spirit and my soul say it's true! I've been born again! I have the victory that is written here. Glory be to God. I have triumphed over sin, and death, and hell, and the grave. God delivered me from the hand of satan unto God by the resurrection power. That same resurrection power that raised Jesus from the dead, resurrected me from the dead, and you from the dead! Because when we were in sin, and sin had dominion over us, we were dead in our trespasses against God.

But when Jesus comes in, God renders self a death blow. That's what water baptism is all about. It's an open show of what already has taken place in the heart. Glory to God, Glory!

And over in Hebrews chapter 1, just a few verses. Verse 7, chapter 1 of Hebrews,

> And of the angels he saith, Who maketh his angels spirits, And his ministers

meaning his angels ministering to us the Saints,

> a flame of fire. But unto the Son he saith, Thy throne, O God, is for ever and ever:

It's forever. It will never decay.

> A sceptre of righteousness is the sceptre of thy kingdom. Thou hast loved righteousness, and hated iniquity;

That's God.

> Therefore God, even thy God, hath anointed thee With the oil of gladness above thy fellows.

If you think that Jesus is somewhere moaning and groaning, not so. He's full of joy. He's full of life. He's full of happiness. He rejoices even far greater than any of us together. Glory to God. That's why he said I will come and sing in the midst of my brethren.

So when we sing, he sings. When you see somebody sing under the anointing of God, that's Jesus singing. That's not just talent. Many people can sing so beautifully. They got great talent to sing, and it's beautiful to the ear. But honey, there's a greater, greater thing, and that's God's anointing upon that singer. That's not just that singer. That's God the Holy Ghost in that singer, singing the glories and the praises of God. Hallelujah!

That's the difference. That's that quickening spirit, you see. Oh, praise our God. Verse 10,

> *And, Thou, Lord, in the beginning hast laid the foundation of the earth;And the heavens are the works of thine hands:*

Dear Jesus!

> *They shall perish;*

The foundation of the earth shall perish,

> *but thou remainest: And they all shall wax old as doth a garment;*

But not Jesus. He's the ancient of days, but if he appears to you, he appears to you as a young 33-year-old man. Glory be to God, because that's how he left here.

Praise our God. Go to Revelation and ask John, How did Jesus appear to him? Hallelujah.

And as a vesture shalt thou fold them up,

He's gonna fold up the Earth. Amen.

And they shall be changed: But thou art the same, And thy years shall not fail.

That's why I say, if he appeared to you, he'll be 33 years old.

But to which of the angels said he at any time, Sit on my right hand, Until I make thine enemies thy footstool?

Here's that footstool again. Jesus is sitting right there until every enemy be brought down, and he's expecting the church to do it. He's expecting us on Earth to get the job done. Hallelujah.

He said Greater works shall you do, because I go to my Father. Hallelujah. We, collectively all over the earth, are shaking satan's kingdom. Amen. That's why the poorest derelict may be the truest, bluest child of God that you could ever see. And they may look like a beggar like Lazarus, not the one that died and rose again, amen, and died again, but the one that Jesus told that is abiding in the bosom of Abraham.

And the rich man fared sumptuously, but bless God, who was the richer after all? That's how we believe. Praise God in the highest… My God, verse 14.

Are they not all ministering spirits, sent forth to minister for them who shall be heirs of salvation?

If you are an heir of salvation, then you have been ministered to by angels. They're spirits, not haints and ghosts and all that nonsense, but true, powerful beings that God has created to minister on our behalf. To keep us in this world, to even keep us from the hour of temptation when the enemy will come against us like a flood, to make us fall. The angels swoop down and undergird us, bear up our feet to keep us from stumbling and falling into sin. Amen.

It's real, why won't you try, God? It's real. This is why we get prayers answered. This is how we get prayers answered. God using his ministering angels and flames of fire to come with the answers to our prayers and deliver them right to us. God sending help from on high. Praise God. He says,

> *Are they not all ministering spirits, sent forth to minister for them who shall be heirs of salvation?*

You see, all the way to the end… are those who are going to receive the inheritance of God's kingdom. Some have started out, some fell by the wayside, but he says, sent forth for them who shall be heirs of salvation. It's not given to the swift nor to the strong. Many start off very fast, some very strong, but God is looking for endurance in each and every one of us. But he that endures to the end shall be saved.

So ask God, if you've fallen by the wayside, Lord, pick me up again. He'll do it. He will do it. He's that God. He's not like man. He'll pick you up, and he'll wash you in his blood. Amen. And he'll treat you like you have never gone back from him. Everything, just like the prodigal son, everything that you had before you left him… is still yours.

All he wants you to do is acknowledge your ways, that they are not pleasing to him. And then come to him, lay that thing at his feet, and let him pick you up and put on you the robe of righteousness. Amen.

Let him cleanse you from the filthiness of the flesh and of the spirit. Let him strengthen you in the power of his might to not fall back again. Glory be to God. And let him love you dearly. Let him be your friend. Let him remain your friend.

Mary Magdalene did. Mary Magdalene was a harlot. But who was there at the tomb? Who saw Jesus first? Mary. Not Mary, the mother of God, but Mary the former harlot. Praise God in the highest. You see the love of God. You see his love. Hallelujah.

Mother Mary, probably somewhere grieving so! Still trying to comprehend what it was all about. What did she birth to? Glory be to God. But Mary Magdalene, cleansed from seven devils that had her living so low. Glory be to God! Those devils cast out of her, her mind made whole, her body cleansed and purified and sanctified. She had every right to see Jesus first! Hallelujah.

Because she remained true to him. What an honor when he said 'Woman.' Glory to God in the highest! You're a part of my being. I honor you this day to see me first. Even before I assent to my father, I just had to present myself to you so you wouldn't grieve and weep any longer, Mary. Now go before me. Go and tell my brethren that I assent to my Father and their Father. To my God and their God.

Precious Jesus. That's how much he loves us. Stop walking around with guilt and hurt, and shame.

Jesus has come to deliver you from such a heavy load of sin. Oh, it feels so good to be free. Feels so good to know that your sins are forgiven, no matter how gross they may be. It feels so good to be cleansed and made a woman or a man, or a child of God. What a mighty God we serve.

Be like the jailer. Sirs, what must we do to be saved? Just repent and keep believing on Jesus Christ. He started out with him. Follow him. Follow him. You might have gotten sidetracked, all right. That's not the end, you're still breathing. You're still here on this side. Amen.

Let him save! Let him deliver you! Let him cleanse and purify you again! Hallelujah. Put him on, wear Jesus. You'll be so free, your mind so rested. Just think what a heaviness it is. How you can't even think clearly anymore. Glory be to God.

I know after I met Jesus, and then I decided I was gonna do things my way, and I tried for three days to do things my way. I've had such a miserable time trying to figure out what I was gonna do with my life and how I was gonna take care of my children. Oh my lord, I was miserable. I was still a young Christian, and I didn't understand God's chastening, and I didn't understand his correction, so I got mad at him and said I wasn't gonna follow him anymore.

And for three days, I tried not to follow him. But every morning, he was such a part of me, I'd wake up, and then I would feel something was wrong. I'd wake up to talk to him… Something's wrong. What is it? What is it? And then I would remember, oh my God. I'm at odds with God.

Well, I'm not gonna do what he said. I don't want to do it. I refuse to do it. And for three days, I walked around stubborn and a fool. And then I couldn't take it anymore. I said Oh God, I can't stand it, it's too heavy. And it was. It was too heavy.

And I made my way back to Jesus. And I've been there ever since. And I tell you, those three days were the worst days I have ever seen in my life. I thought I had a hard time as a sinner. Those three days after knowing him and deliberately being outside of his kingdom were the most miserable days I've ever spent in my life. It's better to stay with Jesus. Amen.

Even if we are stupid and blind and a fool. It is still better to stay with Jesus than to be wise in our own conceit and die outside of him. Glory to his name.

The word of God tells us in Hebrews chapter 2, verse 3,

> *how shall we escape, if we neglect so great salvation; which at the first began to be spoken by the Lord, and was confirmed unto us by them that heard him;*

How shall we escape if we reject him? If we neglect our souls from coming up in him, how shall we escape his judgments? Mercy rejoiceth against judgment. But blessed ones, there is going to come a time, there is a day approaching very soon, that we will not escape the wrath of God or the day of vengeance of our Lord. If we neglect him now and we neglect the care of our souls in his hand, we'll pay for it in the end.

But be wise, don't let that day catch you unprepared like so many, it will, but not say not me, Lord. It will not happen to me. I choose life. As one songwriter, song leader, sings I choose joy. That's life. There's so much, so much concerning him. I could go on and on, but I will not. Don't want to wear your patience, but I do want to share this. In the 11th verse,

> *For both he that sanctifieth and they who are sanctified are all of one:*

Jesus is sanctified, and so are we because we have received him. But in verse 12,

> *saying, I will declare thy name unto my brethren, In the midst of the church will I sing praise unto thee.*

And that's why I mentioned a while ago that Jesus sings in the midst of us.

> *And again, I will put my trust in him. And again, Behold I and the children which God hath given me.*

Remember how Jesus prayed for us in St. John 17? This is the Lord's Prayer?

> *Forasmuch then as the children are partakers of flesh and blood, he also himself likewise took part of the same; that through death he might destroy him that had the power of death, that is, the devil;*

So as far as Jesus is concerned, as far as the Church of God is concerned, satan's already destroyed

> *and deliver them who through fear of death were all their lifetime subject to bondage.*

and that's why we do not fear death, because death is bondage. In verse 17,

Wherefore in all things it behoved him to be made like unto his brethren, that he might be a merciful and faithful high priest in things pertaining to God, to make reconciliation for the sins of the people.

This is who Jesus is. He reconciles. He's merciful. He's forgiving. He's our intercessor.

Amen.

PERFECT UNITY IN CHRIST

First Aired July 17ᵗʰ, 1994

Second Peter, chapter three, verse 9,

> *The Lord is not slack concerning his promise, as some men count slackness; but is longsuffering to us-ward, not willing that any should perish, but that all should come to repentance. But the day of the Lord will come as a thief in the night; in the which the heavens shall pass away with a great noise, and the elements shall melt with fervent heat, the earth also and the works that are therein shall be burned up. Seeing then*

And how many in here see what this writer is saying? How many see and understand? That's what see means.

> Seeing then that all these things shall be dissolved,

The world and the fullness thereof shall be dissolved. Even the elements are going to burn with fervent heat. Do you see this? What he's asking is, and what I'm asking is, do you really understand this? Do you accept this as truth? Praise God, all right.

> *Seeing* then *that* all these things shall be dissolved, what manner *of persons* ought ye to be in *all* holy conversation and godliness,

In all holy conversation and godliness, what manner of persons ought you to be? Amen. In other words, looking at our lives more closely in our daily conduct.

175

looking for and hasting unto the coming of the day of God,

We're supposed to be looking for it and hasting to it, hasting to it! Getting in a hurry! Amen. To get home, to get home…

looking for and hasting unto the coming of the day of God,

meaning God the Son,

wherein the heavens being on fire shall be dissolved, and the elements shall melt with fervent heat?

It's a question…let me go back to verse 11. I don't want your attention divided. I want your attention solely on what is being read here.

Seeing then that all these things shall be dissolved, what manner of persons ought ye to be in all holy conversation and godliness, looking for and hasting unto the coming of the day of God, wherein the heavens being on fire shall be dissolved, and the elements shall melt with fervent heat?

Nevertheless we, according to his promise, look for new heavens and a new earth, wherein dwelleth righteousness.

Wherefore, beloved, seeing that ye look for such things, be diligent

Be diligent…

that ye may be found of him in peace,

glory to God,

without spot, and blameless.

That's how we are to be found. So that means we got to be holy.

Wholly holy, W-h-o-l-l-y. H-o-l-y. Holy, without spot and blameless.

And account that the longsuffering of our Lord is salvation;

And that's what I was telling the man yesterday. I said, it's been the long-suffering of God that has brought us here today. That has brought you to this place of acceptance, long-suffering. And,

even as our beloved brother Paul also according to the wisdom given unto him hath written unto you; as also in all his epistles, speaking in them of these things; in which are some things hard to be understood, which they that are unlearned and unstable wrest,

or wrestle with.

as they do also the other scriptures, unto their own destruction.

In other words, if you're unstable in what God is saying, you're unsound in his word, you're gonna wrestle with his word and not become fruitful. You see? And that's to your own destruction.

Ye therefore, beloved, seeing ye know these things

…which you have witnessed, you see? You acknowledge that you saw, that you understood. Okay?

seeing ye know these things before, beware

When you see that word beware, that's caution, caution. It's a signal of warning.

beware lest ye also, being led away with the error of the wicked, fall from your own stedfastness.

See? Now the only way you keep from falling from your steadfastness is to stop making excuses for the flesh.

'Well, the Lord is merciful,' and 'The Lord is gracious,' and so forth and so on, and when you get in that frame of mind, satan knows that you are willing to allow sin to have preeminence. Because you're gonna take God's mercies for granted and you're gonna come back, 'Lord forgive me', 'Lord forgive me', 'Lord forgive me', and that way you're not steadfast. When you're steadfast, you don't make any leeway for the flesh. Amen.

You're hard on that rascal. You're determined that it's not going to win against you because you're watching for the coming of the Lord that mighty day, and you're hastening unto it in holiness and sobriety and steadfastness. That's victory living.

That's living by the true faith of God. Having faith that God is able to keep you from falling from steadfast hope and the place that God has brought you unto. And we have an adversary, the devil is our adversary, the world is our adversary, the flesh is our adversary. And all three of them conspire together against our living soul to defeat us in our purpose and to defeat us in our steadfast hope.

And that's why with the power of God in us and the Word of God in us, we must stand with the whole armor of God and keep our steadfast place in the Lord. Amen.

satan's entire aim, his whole aim, is to overthrow us from our walk and our place that God has brought us to. He's a thief, and he doesn't always come and cloak us over the head from behind. He'll come right in front of us. That's why Jesus said, Get behind me, satan.

He came right in front of Jesus and tried his subtle tactics. But Jesus remained in prayer. He remained with a prayerful attitude, and he stayed in the presence of his Father because he knew that he is the living Word. And he gave him the Word, and we are abiding in that same living Word. That's where we live in the Word of God. Or do we? Do we live there? Church, do we live in the Word? Is the Word in us?

Well, why are you afraid to say it? If you don't confess him, he will not confess you. Be quick to confess him. He is the living Word. Do you live in him? Glory to God. Long as satan sees you timid like that, he's gonna come and buffet you more. That's the way he works. When the Holy Ghost throws out questions to us like that, God means for us to have a ready answer before him because that proves where we stand.

And when satan sees you shine away, or reluctant to speak, he knows he's got ground and he's coming for it. But God wants us to be so in him that when God speaks, when God asks us a question, and he does, and it's not to catch us, it's to make us aware, to sharpen us of who we are in Christ Jesus. Praise God in the highest.

And if we are abiding in him, we shouldn't be agitated by God desiring to know and bring forth out of us that which he wants to hear. If we don't volunteer it, then God it will stir us up. And he has many ways to do it, to bring forth faith out of our being. Hallelujah. If you believe God to the keeping of your soul, you will say it. Amen.

Because you better believe it, satan is coming after you to make you doubt God and make you doubt your walk with Christ. That's why you've got to check with him every day and hasten unto that coming of the Lord. Praise his holy name.

Let me read verse 15 again,

> And account that the longsuffering of our
> Lord is salvation; even as our beloved brother Paul
> also according to the wisdom given unto him hath
> written unto you;

Okay, verse 17,

> Ye therefore, beloved, seeing ye know these
> things before, beware lest ye also,

Why is that written? To keep us alert, to prod us. Amen.

> being led away with the error of the wicked, fall
> from your own stedfastness. But grow in grace,

Grow! As we knelt here in prayer today, this is what the Lord poured in my heart. I thought I had the message. I really did. And God poured this in my heart to get up and say to you, Amen.

*grow in grace, and in the knowledge of our Lord
and Saviour Jesus Christ.*

Know him. Grow in his grace and grow in his knowledge.

To him be glory both now and for ever. Amen.

To him be glory right now and forevermore. And all heaven
says amen. And the children of God of the earth say amen.
Praise our God. It's a beautiful, beautiful letter written to
the Church of God, Ephesians chapter 4 verse 13. Now he's
talking about the ministries, the fivefold ministries that are
given for the perfection of the saints, the work of the
ministry, for the edifying of the body of Christ, that ye
might grow in his grace and in the knowledge of Jesus
Christ.

And then he says here, verse 13, Ephesians 4:13,

till we all come in the unity of the faith,

God wants us in unity, God wants unity, God wants unity!
Unity is agreement. Action through agreement,

unity of the faith,

And here we go again,

and of the knowledge of the Son of God,

He says till we all come to that place. These ministries are
given. These ministries are given. Teaching ministries,
apostolic ministries, prophetic ministries, pastor ministries,
and evangelistic ministries… all are given till we all come
in the unity of the faith. And that's why we must always be
praying. The Spirit of God is one; preachers should be
preaching the same message. There should be no new
doctrine. There should be no schisms or divisions.

We should be pointing everybody to Jesus Christ. Letting them know that they cannot keep themselves. Jesus did not say, Jesus did not come telling us that, well, because I am merciful and I come to redeem you and to shed my blood for you...You can make mistakes. It's alright. No, he didn't!

I want your attention! He didn't do it! You know what he said? Be perfect! Be ye holy! Be clean! Pray always and endure all things, abide in me. That's what Jesus said. Nothing short of it. We must be overcomers.

The Holy Spirit will make us overcomers if we listen to Him, obey Him, and follow Him.

> *till we all come in the unity of the faith,*

Of the faith, it's only one.

> *and of the knowledge of the Son of God,*

unto a what?

> *unto a perfect man,*

Oh no, no, no, no. It's a mistake here. It's misprinted... That's what the world wants us to think. That's what the flesh wants us to believe. That's what the devil would rejoice in if we embrace. But until we become fully believers in all that God says unto a perfect man...

And here's what the Holy Spirit poured in my heart. Grow in grace and this latter part here,

> *unto the measure of the stature of the fulness of Christ:*

That's how we are to grow up. And we won't do it as long as our attention is short-spanned in his presence. We must think, Jesus. We must eat Jesus. We must be baptized in Jesus every day of our lives. Bathe in him that we might grow up in him and in the knowledge of him.

If we only look to Jesus as our Savior and our provider and our protection, we're not gonna grow. We will not grow. We cannot grow. We will not grow up into the full stature of who he is. We can't do it if we don't see him as he is.

He's more than our Savior. He's more than our divine protection. He's God, and we got to see what that means. So we got to stay in his presence. Come after him. Say,

> "Lord, make yourself known to me. I want to know you. I want a closer relationship with you…"

And be prepared to die. Be prepared to die to yourself because God is gonna pinpoint what's hindering your relationship and your fellowship with him. And unless you're willing to die, forget about knowing him. Forget about the knowledge of Jesus Christ because you won't know it. He reveals his secrets to those that love him. Amen.

Let's read it again together. Verse 13, Ephesians 4,

> *till we all come in the unity of the faith, and of the knowledge of the Son of God, unto a perfect man, unto the measure of the stature of the fulness of Christ:*

Not a portion, precious ones, but the fullness of Christ. Measure of the stature of the fullness of Christ. Are you willing? Are you willing to be brought there by the Holy Ghost because he's the only one who's gonna get you there?

Are you willing to follow him? Are you willing to be baptized in him? Are you willing to obey the Holy Spirit? He will not lead you astray. He will not lead you into a different doctrine. He will lead you unto Jesus, and he'll be your bread. He'll be your strength. He'll be the power you need. Praise God. He'll be that fullness because he is, He is fullness.

It's in him that all the fullness of the God head, body, dwelleth. It's in Jesus. It's in Jesus. The Father's eyes are on Jesus. The Holy Ghost takes us right to Jesus. That's where the fullness is.

So be determined that you are going to grow in the grace and in the knowledge of Jesus Christ. Aren't you tired of being stunted? Praise God. Don't you want to win? Aren't you tired of yourself? Well, abhor it! Amen. And go after God. Say,

> "Lord, I'm breaking out of this prison. Loose me from the shackle of self. Set me free. Set me in the liberty of the Holy Spirit. I'm coming after you."

And come after him. Amen! Anytime the Holy Ghost moves on you, in that time when you don't want to be disturbed, and he moves on you, move with him! Move with him and you'll see some growing in your life. God wants growth here, and this is the only way you're going to grow.

Psalms 85.

> *LORD, thou hast been favourable unto thy land:*
>
> *Thou hast brought back the captivity of Jacob.*
>
> *Thou hast forgiven the iniquity of thy people,*

Thou hast covered all their sin. Selah.

Thou hast taken away all thy wrath:

Thou hast turned thyself from the fierceness of thine anger.

Turn us, O God of our salvation,

And cause thine anger toward us to cease.

Wilt thou be angry with us for ever?

Wilt thou draw out thine anger to all generations?

Wilt thou not revive us again:

That thy people may rejoice in thee?

Shew us thy mercy, O LORD,

And grant us thy salvation.

I will hear what God the LORD will speak:

For he will speak peace unto his people, and to his saints: But let them not turn again to folly.

Surely his salvation is nigh them that fear him;

That glory may dwell in our land.

Mercy and truth are met together;

Righteousness and peace have kissed each other.

Truth shall spring out of the earth;

And righteousness shall look down from heaven.

Yea, the LORD shall give that which is good;

And our land shall yield her increase.

That's growth, that's growth!

> *Righteousness shall go before him;*
>
> *And shall set us in the way of his steps.*

Oh, bless the Lord! Bless the Lord! Bless the Lord! Bless your name, O Lord! Praise the Lord of hosts. We thank you for your promises! These are promises. They're yea and amen to them that fear him. Glory to God in the highest. Hallelujah.

KNOW GOD (PART 1)

First Aired April 9th, 2000

Glory to God in the highest. What a privilege it is to come your way again by the way of radio, and we give God the praise and the honor because certainly it is due unto Him always. This is your evangelist, Martha P. Davis, bringing you the word of life.

I give God the honor in speaking His word faithfully, those things that He's put upon my heart to make manifest unto you. It's an honor, it's always an honor to glorify His name before the children of men. And surely, I thank God for this privilege that He entrusted me with His word, to speak His word, to make known His desires to the children of men.

What a privilege, and what a privilege it is to hear the word of God. Faith cometh by hearing and hearing by the word of God, magnificent Father that He is. Let us pray.

Lord, we give honor to Your name. We give honor to all that You are, for surely You are high and lifted up. And we glory in Your name today. Take preeminence over us all. We thank You for the privilege, Lord, to come into Your presence. We thank You, Lord, for blessing us to come into Your presence.

Thank You for the access to the throne of grace. Glory to God, thank You, Lord, for all the work that You have accomplished on this earth that we can come boldly to the throne of grace and find Your mercies to help us in the time of need. Lord, I ask Your blessings upon Your people today.

And most of all, I ask Your blessings upon Your word as You direct Your word into the hearts of Your people. Be glorified in us all for Thy namesake and for Thy honor. And bind the forces of hell that would come to steal the word of God.

We bind the thief, the robber, and the killer today. In the authority and the power of Jesus' name, glory, hallelujah. And we lose, Lord, thy sanctification, we lose thy power to work in the lives of your people. Glory to God, have Your mighty way. We ask these blessings in the authority of Your name, amen and amen.

In the 17th chapter of St. John, it reads,

> *These words spake Jesus, and lifted up his eyes to heaven, and said, Father, the hour is come; glorify thy Son, that thy Son also may glorify thee: as thou hast given him power over all flesh,*

And I want to emphasize this.

> *as thou hast given him power over all flesh, that he should give eternal life to as many as thou hast given him. And this is life eternal, that they might know thee the only true God, and Jesus Christ, whom thou hast sent.*

And this is life eternal, that they might know Thee, the only true God, and Jesus Christ, whom Thou hast sent. This is the will of God for every one of us, is to know who God is, the true God, the almighty creator. And more than this, He says, Jesus says, this is life eternal. In other words, what we know about God brings life eternal.

This is why God sent the Son… to reveal the Father unto us. Remember the 14th chapter of St. John, Jesus was talking about heaven, and one asked Him, Lord, show us the Father. And Jesus said, What? Have I not been all this time with you, and you have not seen the Father? When you have seen me, you have seen the Father.

In other words, Jesus was letting them know that I came to the earth to manifest the Father to you, to reveal who God the Father is to you. The God of all creation desires to be your Father, your Father. And I came to make reconciliation between you and the Father, or the Father and you.

You see, sin had separated mankind from God, as it does today. But Jesus came, came to bring, to bridge that gap, to bring life eternal. And the way He did it was to manifest the Father, to reveal the Father to the children of men.

And He emphasizes this, as thou hast given Him power over all flesh, that He should give eternal life to as many as thou hast given Him. You see, everyone, and this is sad, everyone is not given or not purposed to serve God. That's not God's fault. That's the will of man.

Many will not believe God. It's those that believe when they hear the gospel, when they hear the truth. Jesus said, My sheep know My voice. We know the truth. He is the Spirit of truth. He is truth, praise His holy name. And then Jesus goes on to say in verse 4,

> *I have glorified thee on the earth: I have finished the work which thou gavest me to do.*

That which You sent Me to do, He is speaking. As a matter of fact, it's just a few days left that Jesus will be crucified.

But He is speaking as if the work is already done, because that is the reason He came. To die that we might live. To shed His blood that we might be justified. What great love. And what manifestation of the love of God for all the world. He says,

> *And now, O Father, glorify thou me with thine own self with the glory which I had with thee before the world was.*

Before the world was spoken into existence, before the world was created, glorify thou Me, with the same glory, the glory that I had with You from the beginning, which I had with Thee before the world was.

And that makes me believe that when God the Father said, Let us make man in the book of Genesis, He was referring to His Son. He said,

> *I have manifested thy name unto the men which thou gavest me out of the world:*

Out of, separated, born into the world, but brought unto God out of the world.

> *thine they were, and thou gavest them me; and they have kept thy word.*

Glorify means to praise, honor, and worship God. To make glorious light or splendor. It means to throw a glorious light upon, to give radiance. And that's what Jesus came to do. The word of life manifested to the children of men, to those whom God had given Him.

And He spoke the word of God freely, freely to all that would listen. But not everyone believed. It was those that believed God that were able to see this glorious light.

That basked themselves in the radiance of God, in the beauty of God's holiness. That's what the Lord meant, and He still means today. Glorify Thou Me.

And He glorified the Father. He purposely and faithfully glorified God the Father unto the children of men. And they wanted to stone Him to death because He did it.

He said that He was with God, that before the world was, He was with God. And they wanted to stone Him because He also said before Abraham was, I am. He said the people accused Him of blasphemy.

They accused Him of lying and calling Himself equal with God. And indeed He is, because He is God the Son. And He was manifested in the flesh by God and the Holy Spirit.

Holy God, my rock. To glory means to great praise and honor, fame, renown, source of pride and joy. And this we have in the Father. The psalmist says My soul shall make her boast in the Lord. In the Lord. Hallelujah. A thing of radiant beauty or magnificence… or magnificence. This is who God is.

And this is who Jesus revealed to those that loved God, that heard the Word. Only those that hear the Word of God can see the glory of God. Faith arises in the heart. For they choose to believe. And God manifests Himself to those who believe. Only to those that believe.

Now Jesus says,

> *I have manifested thy name unto the men which*
> *thou gavest me out of the world: thine they were,*

and thou gavest them me; and they have kept thy
word.

See how important it is when we hear the Word of God.
Believe it and do it.

> *Now they have known that all things whatsoever*
> *thou hast given me are of thee.*

All the Word that You have given me, whatsoever You have
given me. They have known that I have spoken the truth.
And that You have given me to speak these things to them.
This is what He's really saying. He's talking to the Father.
While those who love Him are standing by, listening to
Jesus praying. Now this is truly the Lord's Prayer. What we
call the Lord's Prayer is really Jesus teaching us to pray.

It's called the Disciple's Prayer. But this is the Lord's
Prayer. And He says in verse 8,

> *For I have given unto them the words which thou*
> *gavest me; and they have received them, and have*
> *known surely that I came out from thee,*

Have known… they have known, surely. Without a doubt,
no place for unbelief. They

> *have known surely that I came out from thee, and*
> *they have believed that thou didst send me.*

They believed…Oh, how glorious that is. To believe every
word that proceeds out of the mouth of God, is a glorious
and mighty blessing that only God can give. What a mighty
thing to do.

And what a mighty place to be in, to believe God's every
word. Every word, Not what we want to hear, not choosing

some of Christ's words, and allowing others to slip by. But He said,

> *For I have given unto them the words which thou gavest me; and they have received them, and have known surely that I came out from thee, and they have believed that thou didst send me.*

You sent me. And those that You have given me, Believed. And He's saying the same thing today. The Word of God is in effect today. As it was when Jesus stood praying this prayer. Before His departure from the earth, physically.

And this is why the Gospel of Jesus Christ is going throughout the world today. Being made manifest to those that belong to God. Even though they are sinning, they are sinners yet. But when they hear the Word, they come to God. For the powerful Word of God draws them. The Word of God is powerful.

Praise the Living God. I love His Word. Glory to His Name. He says in verse 9,

> *I pray for them: I pray not for the world, but for them which thou hast given me; for they are thine. And all mine are thine, and thine are mine; and I am glorified in them.*

And all mine are Thine, and Thine are mine. In other words, whatever is yours, it's mine also. Oh, what a great relationship of love. And it's the same with us. For the Lord has manifested God the Father, God our Maker, God of all creation, to us. And He calls Him, Our Father... Our Father.

> *And all mine are thine, and thine are mine; and I am glorified in them.*

I am honored in them. I am manifested unto them. And they honor me because Thou hast sent me. And they have known surely that You have sent me. Oh, what a mighty loving prayer. For every one of us today.

Isn't it a marvelous place to be in? That we belong to God? And that God loves us so much that He recalls Jesus Christ to pray such a priestly prayer. For everyone that believes. Not for the world, because the world does not believe. It's for those that God has called from the world, us.

He says,

> *And now I am no more in the world, but these are in the world,*

We're still here.

> *and I come to thee. Holy Father,*

He just doesn't say Father, but he says, Holy Father.

> *keep through thine own name those whom thou hast given me, that they may be one, as we are. While I was with them in the world, I kept them in thy name:*

While I was with them...

> *those that thou gavest me I have kept,*

In other words. None of us will slip from His hand. No man is able. And no power is able to pluck us out of God's hands. Hallelujah.

He said,

> *those that thou gavest me I have kept, and none of them is lost, but the son of perdition;*

Meaning Judas, the one that betrayed Him, the one that betrayed innocent blood. He said,

> but the son of perdition; that the scripture might be fulfilled.

What is written here shall be fulfilled, everything that is written in the word of God, that's prophesied, it shall be fulfilled. Not one jot, not tittle of the word of God shall pass until all be fulfilled. So Judas had to fulfill the word of God, because it was already prophesied in the scriptures. That there would be one who would betray Him, proving that God knows the end from the beginning. The Lord goes on to pray,

> While I was with them in the world, I kept them in thy name: those that thou gavest me I have kept, and none of them is lost, but the son of perdition; that the scripture might be fulfilled. And now come I to thee;

I'm coming home, Father.

> and these things I speak in the world, that they might have my joy fulfilled in themselves.

I speak it before them. I pray this prayer before them, that they may know my joy. And my joy might be fulfilled in them. He says,

> I have given them thy word;

Oh, what faithfulness. That's why Jesus is called true and faithful.

I have given them thy word; and the world hath hated them, because they are not of the world, even as I am not of the world.

When the Lord brings us out. And he causes us to be born again by his Spirit. He lifts us up from the beggarly, weakly things of this world, and the false pleasures of this world. And he puts heaven in us. He puts God the Father and God the Son, and God the Holy Spirit in us. He puts the desire of God in us, and it's greater than this world. He says,

I pray not that thou shouldest take them out of the world, but that thou shouldest keep them from the evil.

Keep them from the temptations of the devil. Keep them from the lust of this world. And the pride of this worldly life. What a magnificent prayer.

They are not of the world, even as I am not of the world.

And this is why the world looks on us and despises us; they hate us because we are not like they are. And it's because of the work of the Lord God creator in us, moving in us. Because we dare to believe the truth.

It pays to believe the truth. And here's what the Lord says,

Sanctify them through thy truth: thy word is truth.

The meaning of Sanctify: Holiness of life, holy character, sacredness, to set apart as sacred. Observe as holy.

Consecrate: To make a person free from sin. To make right. To justify.

Sanctification: The art of sanctifying or making holy.

And this is what the Lord is praying. For all that will come to him. Sanctify them through the truth. Continue to make them holy, continue to keep them separate. From the evil of this world. And from the bondage of sin. Bring them into the sacredness of thy holy word.

Sanctify them through thy truth: thy word is truth.

And this is what Jesus says in the 15th chapter, verse 5,

I am the vine, ye are the branches: He that abideth in me, and I in him, the same bringeth forth much fruit: for without me ye can do nothing. If a man abide not in me, he is cast forth as a branch, and is withered; and men gather them, and cast them into the fire, and they are burned.

If ye abide in me, and my words abide in you, ye shall ask what ye will, and it shall be done unto you. Herein is my Father glorified, that ye bear much fruit; so shall ye be my disciples.

See, it's conditional. It's believing God's word and abiding in it. And this is where satan brings the big lie, that we cannot keep God's word. That we can't help but fall because we are human. No, we were… but now we have become superhuman.

Because the holy God of heaven and earth abides in us. He sups with us and we with the Godhead body. This is what sacredness is. This is what sanctification is. We cannot underestimate the power of God in keeping us unto Himself. Keeping us from the evil of this world.

Don't underestimate God's keeping power, precious ones. Do not listen to those who do not know God. They speak their own minds like the Pharisees and the Sadducees of old. But God has a people that believe the word of God. All of it. And that God is able to keep that which is committed unto him. Bless his holy name.

In 2 Thessalonians chapter 2. Beginning at the 13th verse, here's what it says,

> *But we are bound to give thanks alway to God for you, brethren beloved of the Lord, because God hath from the beginning chosen you to salvation through sanctification of the Spirit and belief of the truth:*

See, it all hangs on our believing the truth. Jesus said, I am the way, the truth, and the life. What I speak unto you, it is true.

> *whereunto he called you by our gospel, to the obtaining of the glory of our Lord Jesus Christ.*

We have obtained the glory of the Lord, and it is revealed unto us. Let me read it again,

> *But we are bound to give thanks alway to God for you, brethren beloved of the Lord, because God hath from the beginning chosen you to salvation through sanctification of the Spirit and belief of the truth:*
>
> *whereunto he called you by our gospel, to the obtaining of the glory of our Lord Jesus Christ. Therefore, brethren, stand fast, and hold the traditions which ye have been taught, whether by word, or our epistle.*

Hold fast to the word and let no man weaken you. Let no man give you their own interpretation.

Let the Holy Spirit reveal the truth to you. This is called knowing God. Know Him. It's the word of God. And to know God is power. Sweet fellowship with Him.

That's what we're called to sanctification. Knowing Him, learning Him, learning His thoughts, learning His ways. And putting Him on. The word of God says, Put on the Lord Jesus Christ. Put Him on. This is holiness.

Oh, it's a beautiful walk. And God is calling us all unto it. For when Jesus comes, this is what He's looking for. And this is what's going to catch us up to meet Him in the air. It shall surely be. And those that love Him, the world hates us. The world despises us because we speak His truth.

And we live accordingly. According to that, which God makes manifest unto us by His Spirit. And He says in John 17:19,

> *And for their sakes I sanctify myself, that they also might be sanctified through the truth.*

God's word belongs to you, and you belong to God. God bless you. Amen.

KNOW GOD (PART 2)

First Aired April 16th, 2000

Greetings, everyone. Thank God for Jesus Christ. Thank God for this glorious day that he has made, and we shall rejoice and be glad in it, for the Lord hath made it for his glory, and he hath made us that we might glorify his name.

I thank God for his word today, and I'll be ministering from John chapter 20, also from 1st Corinthians 15. You that have your Bibles and Radio Land, please listen attentively as we go into the word of God. First of all, let us pray.

Father, we thank you for this glorious day, this day that you have made, each one celebrating the resurrection of Jesus Christ. It's a marvellous thing to celebrate, because it is our life. Jesus rose from the dead that we might live, and that we might live victoriously and abundantly in the grace of God.

Thank you for sending Jesus, for taking our place, Lord Jesus, we thank you. At Calvary, you bore our sins upon your body on that rugged tree, that we might have life everlasting, that we might be justified before God, our maker. Thank you for the blood that you shed, for you said in your word, Lord, without the shedding of blood, there should be no remission of sin.

But you have remitted our sins, because you hung on that cross. You were made sin for us, not that you had done anything wrong. You had done no sin, Lord Jesus.

But because of what you took upon yourself, our sins, you were made sin. You bore our transgressions on Calvary. Glory to your name. We are ever grateful. We are ever thankful. We thank you for loving us so much and loving the Father that you would obey him even unto death.

Thank you for going into hell and destroying the powers of darkness, for taking the keys of death, hell, and the grave. Thank you for triumphing and rising again from the dead, that we might live victoriously. What a mighty God we serve.

We give you honor. We give you praise for all that you've done for us. And thank you that you are coming again to receive us unto yourself, that where you are, we shall be. We shall live with you forever. Thank you, Lord, for this hope that you put within us. Hope maketh not ashamed.

Thank you for the privilege to live victoriously. In your name, thank you for the power that's in your name, Lord Jesus. And thank you for the faith that you've given us. Thank you for calling us to be your very own. Praise your holy name for taking our place, for being life while we were dead, and dying for us that we might live. Praise your name.

Thank you for all the days of our lives. We do thank you, and we bless your name forever. Amen and amen.

The 20th chapter of John. This is after Jesus had risen from the dead.

> *The first day of the week cometh Mary Magdalene early, when it was yet dark, unto the sepulchre, and seeth the stone taken away from the sepulchre. Then*

*she runneth, and cometh to Simon Peter, and to the
other disciple, whom Jesus loved,*

meaning John,

*and saith unto them, They have taken away the Lord
out of the sepulchre, and we know not where they
have laid him. Peter therefore went forth, and that
other disciple, and came to the sepulchre.*

That's the place where they had buried Jesus, had laid his
body.

*So they ran both together: and the other disciple did
outrun Peter, and came first to the sepulchre. And
he stooping down, and looking in, saw the linen
clothes lying; yet went he not in. Then cometh
Simon Peter following him, and went into the
sepulchre, and seeth the linen clothes lie, and the
napkin, that was about his head, not lying with the
linen clothes, but wrapped together in a place by
itself.*

*Then went in also that other disciple, which came
first to the sepulchre, and he saw, and believed.*

In our last broadcast, we talked about believing, believing
the Word of God, how powerful it is to believe the Word of
the Lord. When the disciples, John and Peter, saw that
Jesus was not in the tomb, they believed.

They had begun to remember that Jesus said he would rise
again. This is what they believed.

For as yet they knew not the scripture, that he must rise again from the dead. Then the disciples went away again unto their own home.

But Mary stood without at the sepulchre weeping: and as she wept, she stooped down, and looked into the sepulchre, and seeth two angels in white sitting, the one at the head, and the other at the feet, where the body of Jesus had lain. And they say unto her, Woman, why weepest thou? She saith unto them, Because they have taken away my Lord, and I know not where they have laid him.

Now, none of these disciples, not even Mary Magdalene's understanding, was fruitful at the time. But Jesus, in his tenderness, was willing to reveal himself because of their love for him and especially Mary. She says,

And when she had thus said, she turned herself back, and saw Jesus standing, and knew not that it was Jesus. Jesus saith unto her, Woman, why weepest thou? whom seekest thou? She, supposing him to be the gardener, saith unto him, Sir, if thou have borne him hence, tell me where thou hast laid him, and I will take him away. Jesus saith unto her, Mary. She turned herself, and saith unto him, Rabboni; which is to say, Master.

Jesus saith unto her, Touch me not; for I am not yet ascended to my Father: but go to my brethren, and say unto them, I ascend unto my Father, and your Father; and to my God, and your God.

You see the oneness? I ascend unto my Father and your Father, and to my God and your God.

*Mary Magdalene came and told the disciples that
she had seen the Lord, and that he had spoken these
things unto her.*

*Then the same day at evening, being the first day of
the week, when the doors were shut where the
disciples were assembled for fear of the Jews, came
Jesus and stood in the midst, and saith unto
them, Peace be unto you.*

*And when he had so said, he shewed unto
them his hands and his side. Then were the disciples
glad, when they saw the Lord. Then said Jesus to
them again, Peace be unto you: as my Father hath
sent me, even so send I you.*

And this is what Jesus prayed in the 17th chapter of St.
John.

*And when he had said this, he breathed on them,
and saith unto them, Receive ye the Holy
Ghost: whose soever sins ye remit, they are remitted
unto them; and whose soever sins ye retain, they are
retained.*

*But Thomas, one of the twelve, called Didymus, was
not with them when Jesus came. The other disciples
therefore said unto him, We have seen the Lord. But
he said unto them, Except I shall see in his hands
the print of the nails, and put my finger into the
print of the nails, and thrust my hand into his side, I
will not believe.*

That's the choice God gives every person. He gives us a
will to believe or not believe. And Didymus was faithful to
carry out that which God had given him. Not that it was

pleasing to God, God had given him freedom of choice. And he was faithful to use his freedom of choice. But it was not good for him. Verse 26,

> *And after eight days again his disciples were within, and Thomas with them: then came Jesus, the doors being shut, and stood in the midst, and said, Peace be unto you.*
>
> *Then saith he to Thomas, Reach hither thy finger, and behold my hands; and reach hither thy hand, and thrust it into my side: and be not faithless, but believing. And Thomas answered and said unto him, My Lord and my God.*
>
> *Jesus saith unto him, Thomas, because thou hast seen me, thou hast believed: blessed are they that have not seen, and yet have believed.*
>
> *And many other signs truly did Jesus in the presence of his disciples, which are not written in this book: but these are written, that ye might believe that Jesus is the Christ, the Son of God; and that believing ye might have life through his name.*

I read those verses in chapter 20, that you might have a good understanding, as we read in Corinthians, 1st Corinthians chapter 15. Here is one Paul speaking in chapter 15 of 1st Corinthians. He was the one consenting unto Stephen's death, one of the Lord's disciples later in life. Stephen himself had not seen Jesus personally or had not handled Jesus like the 12 had. He became a disciple later in life.

He was a chosen one, full of the Holy Ghost, full of the wisdom and fear of God, full of the power of God, able to preach the word of God. Yet he was a deacon, found faithful and just to be entrusted to take care of the widows of his day. Praise God.

But one day, he was charged by the Holy Ghost to preach to those that stood by, questioning who Jesus is. And Stephen began to preach from the very beginning of the book up until his present time as to who Jesus is. And they became pricked in their hearts, the Holy Ghost convicting them of their sins, because they were the children of those who had killed the prophets of old.

So they gnashed upon Stephen, they bit him, they stoned him. They became raging lunatics, maniacs, because of the truth. Remember what Jesus said in Saint John 17, the world shall hate you because you are not of the world, because you believe in me, they shall hate you. And because of that hatred, they killed Stephen, they stoned him to death.

But before Stephen departed, before his spirit left his body, he saw Jesus. He looked up, stoned and bleeding to death, and he looks up into heaven and he sees Jesus Christ, the resurrected Christ, standing up to receive him. Hallelujah. And he said unto him, Lay not this sin to their charge, because he knew they were ignorant. He knew they were blind to the truth, just like Didymus was.

Jesus had preached the truth; he had taught his disciples that he would rise again, that he would have to be put to death for the entire world, but he would rise again victoriously. And Judas was the one that betrayed him.

But Didymus, Thomas, didn't believe. The others believed and yet were blinded to the full truth. Mary, because of her great love for Jesus, Jesus manifested himself to her, even though he had not ascended to the Father to glorify him in reality.

But he said, Go to the brethren and tell them I ascend to your God, your Father, my Father, your Father, my God, your God. And in the time that Mary Magdalene got the message to the disciples, Jesus was in the presence of God the Father. And then he comes, walks right on through, bolted doors… walls, walks unto the brethren and said, peace be unto you. What a mighty God.

That's what he's all about in this world, to bring us peace, peace in the Lord. And when we believe there is peace, no matter what the trouble is, there is peace. The disciples were bolted behind doors that were locked, jammed, actually, to keep those that had persecuted and destroyed, they thought, Jesus Christ. And because of fear, they could not believe. Fear is a tormenting thing; it must be destroyed. It must be done away with, that we might see the glory of God, praise his holy name.

So Jesus walks through the wall, into the midst of the brethren, the disciples, and says, Peace be unto you. And then a few days later, eight days later, after Thomas had heard that Jesus was alive, he said, I will not believe until I see him for myself. I've got to see what I saw as he was crucified. I want to see the nail prints, I want to feel, I want to see it for myself, where he was pierced in his side. When I see that, then I'll believe.

And Jesus walks in and says, Peace be unto you. Now, can you imagine Thomas having peace when Jesus walks in and says, Thomas, come hither, come to me. Give me your hand, thrust it here, put it in my side, and be not faithless, but believing. 'I want to see' (he said). This is not my way, but I'm going to submit to you. I'm going to show you. The others didn't ask, but when they saw me, they believed.

But you want to see, you want to see the proof, Thomas? Okay, come. And Thomas got what he said, that he would not believe unless he saw. See how Jesus is willing to go the extra mile to bring us unto faith, believing that we might have him in the fullness, in the fullness.

We are not full in Christ, and neither is Christ full in us when we are doubting, when we are doubting. But Thomas said, My Lord and my God. Jesus said, Because you have seen, you believe. Blessed are they who have not seen yet believe.

And that brings us to that blessedness today. We didn't see, but when we heard the truth, when we heard the powerful truth, the truth became alive in our hearts, and we believed. And this is why we are saved today, because we came to him like the disciples came to him of old. And here we are, having never put our hands in his nail-scarred hands, never have we put our hands in his side, but we believe. And because we believe, we are alive today.

Heaven is in us, and we are abiding in heaven because as Jesus is, so are we. Remember when Jesus came and started his ministry of reconciliation? Remember what he said, repent ye for the kingdom of heaven is at hand. Thank God for repentance. That's all God requires, repent and believe the gospel, because it is our life, our destiny, really.

What we believe determines where we are to live eternally. Praise his holy name. Thank God for the gift of faith. Thank God for the fruit of faith. But it takes the gift of faith in the beginning to believe the gospel. Not everyone will have this gift because everyone will not believe.

Remember St. John 17, Jesus said, I pray not for the world, but for those thou hast given me out of the world. And he also prayed for us that would believe those that stood with him, that we would believe their gospel. That we would believe their report of Jesus Christ.

Can you imagine the joy that was set ablaze in their hearts when they realized, in the fullness, the things that Jesus had spoken to them? And here it is, right before their eyes, being fulfilled. They were no longer afraid behind bolted doors. But when the Lord Jesus was ascending back to heaven, back to his glory with the Father, the fullness of his Father. He said, Go to the upper room and tarry there. You wait there until you be endued with power from on high, power to get the job done, power to get my message out to the ends of the world, power to demonstrate my love.

And they went, they didn't go afraid any longer. They went rejoicing. They went with hope. They went in faith, believing for this power to be shed upon them, to come upon them. They waited in faith. And after many days, this power came through, Glory be to God!

The Bible says they were baptized in the Holy Ghost and that with fire! Fire, because Jesus, not only the savior of the world, but the baptizer with fire. Praise the Lord God of hosts. And God wants us to know this fire, this fire that comes from God Almighty.

Hallelujah. Fire baptized. It's all right to be baptized in water. Thank God for water, but we need the fire. We need another baptism.

And one time… that's good, that's the initial baptism, but we need it every day of our lives. Look at what's around us. Look at how gross this world has become in darkness. We need this baptism. We need to ask the Lord constantly, fill me through and through with the power of the Holy Ghost, and God will do it. He will refresh your bowels in him.

This is what he wants. He doesn't want us to grow stale on yesteryear, on the initial blessings and outpouring of his spirit. He wants us fresh in the Lord, fresh anointing, fresh oil from on high that we might live victoriously. Praise the Lord of hosts. Glory to God. Here's what Paul says in the 15th chapter of First Corinthians. He says, verse nine,

> *For I am the least of the apostles, that am not meet to be called an apostle, because I persecuted the church of God.*

He did it in ignorance,

> *But by the grace of God I am what I am: and his grace which was bestowed upon me was not in vain; but I laboured more abundantly than they all: yet not I, but the grace of God which was with me. Therefore whether it were I or they, so we preach, and so ye believed.*

> *Now if Christ be preached that he rose from the dead, how say some among you that there is no resurrection of the dead?*

And he goes on to make that known. But he says,

and if Christ be not raised,

verse 17,

> *your faith is vain; ye are yet in your sins. Then they also which are fallen asleep in Christ are perished. If in this life only we have hope in Christ, we are of all men most miserable.*

> *But now is Christ risen from the dead, and become the firstfruits of them that slept.*

Christ is risen. He is alive, and he shall never die.

> *For since by man came death, by man came also the resurrection of the dead. For as in Adam all die, even so in Christ shall all be made alive.*

And that's what Christ is all about: to make us alive unto God by his Spirit. This is what the celebration of Easter is all about, or the celebration of him rising from the dead. He defeated satan, and death has no victory over us.

We are not afraid of death, for Jesus has power over all the power of the enemy, even death, glory to his name. We have the victory triumphant, and Christ wants us to walk in his victory. Do it by the grace of God, and you shall live eternally in his power.

Amen. Amen.

HUMILITY IN JESUS CHRIST

First Aired August 28, 1988

The true Christian who desires to please the Lord always make preparation to meet Jesus. Every day that we live, we are preparing to meet Jesus. Because one day God is going to send him. One day, the Father will say, Son, go get your bride.

Bring her home to me. And the bride of Christ is the church of the living God worldwide. Those who know him in the pardon of their sins and know him in the fellowship of his sufferings.

And that's why I love that song that Colleen was singing. Jesus says through Peter, if we suffer with him, we shall reign with him. And he told us to be of good cheer, no matter what we have to go through in this world, be of good cheer.

And it seems like the church is giving the Holy Ghost a round for it. He's offering us cheer and happiness, joy, peace. That's what's in the Holy Ghost. Peace, joy, and happiness. And we are saying, no, no, no, no, I want to be sad. I want to grumble, I want to murmur, I want to complain.

The Lord is saying that's not the victory. The victory is joy, peace, and happiness. Thank God because that joy is our strength. This is what the enemy of our souls, the devil, hates. He hates joy. You see, he lost joy, he lost his peace. He lost the thrill of his happiness in knowing that he was created holy and that he was a beautiful specimen in the sight of God. He lost all of that.

He lost eternal life with God Almighty, his creator. He wasn't born as you and I. He was created holy and without fault, without sin. And yet in his heart, he decided that he would rise up above God, his maker, his creator, and overthrow his kingdom.

Very foolish, very dumb, most unwise. And because of it, God cast him out as lightning. Jesus said, I beheld satan as lightning fall from heaven. So he's lost. He's reserved unto fetters and chains and darkness forever and ever and ever. No more chance to get right with God…but we have.

Every day that we live, we have a chance, another chance to draw closer, to draw nigh unto God. And you know how that's done? The Bible says we are brought nigh unto God by the blood of Jesus Christ.

It's by the blood. See, it's the blood that will cover us, that the Father will not allow his vengeance and wrath to fall upon us. Only if we are covered, sheltered under the blood of Jesus.

I wish the world could have heard the message Friday night. It was marvelous. The Lord just sat us down and taught us what it is to ask in the name of Jesus, what it truly means to ask the Father anything in his name.

Praise God. And the Lord revealed to us that it's not just merely asking in the name of Jesus, our power of attorney, but it's in the might and within the realm of that name. And we know what that name consists of.

It's holy, it's righteous, it's true. And anything that is not of the truth of God, we cannot ask the Father for. Anything that is not of the righteousness of the Father, we cannot ask the Father for. It has to be within the realm of the name. Everything that he stands for, anything outside of what he stands for, whatever we ask, it's amiss. It's amiss, it's in vain.

So this is why we must study the Word. We must take upon this yoke (the Word of God), bind ourselves to it. Amen. And thoroughly search it out daily to find out who Jesus is, what he consists of, and what is his mind. The Bible says we have the mind of Christ, so we must know what is his mind.

How does he think? What does he reason? And everything that we can come up with, we can ask for that in his name. Amen. And it just went on and on.

And I tell you, the more he taught us, the more thrilled I became. And the more the faith of God was built in my heart, and I'm sure the others that were in the midst. And I tell you, Friday night it was shouting down time.

We didn't roll the rug back. But bless God, the rug stayed intact. But I tell you, our feet were bouncing. Praise God, it was shouting time. Amen. I don't mind dancing before my God. I used to stay on the dance floor for the enemy before I met my God. But now it's for Jesus. And I don't mind dancing before him. Praise God in the highest. Thank you, Jesus. Turn with me to the third chapter of St. Matthew. Praise God in the highest.

We thank the Lord for everyone that are here today, everyone, visitors, and our friends, and of course, the regulars. Amen. We thank God for every one of you. And I know your coming will not be in vain if you came to meet Jesus, because he's here. Praise God.

And I have a very important lesson to teach today. I have one of the most important messages that I'll ever minister to the bride of Christ this day. And I hope everyone is of the bride of Christ. It's important, most important. Without this message, we'll never enter the kingdom of God. That's how grossly important it is. Without this message abiding in us, we'll never enter the kingdom of heaven. We'll never go home to be with Jesus. So, cause your ears to hear what the Spirit of the Lord saith unto the church.

Praise God in the highest. Father, send your word by the power and the action of the Holy Ghost. Anoint your word, Lord God. Let it fall on good ground. We've heard the testimonies of your mercies and your mighty deliverance in bringing forth from the dead and near unto death, Lord.

How you brought salvation to those, Lord God, that longed for you, you longed to know who you were, but yet rejected your mercies. Father, you ran after them anyway because your mercies are great and your mercies are good and your mercies are true. Lord, this is your mercy today that you represent to us through thy word, thy guidance, thy direction unto our path.

Show us clearly. Move the scales from our eyes. Anoint our eyes that we might see, Lord Jesus. You told us in the Word, in the book of Revelation, anoint your eyes with eye salve. We need them anointed. We need our ears anointed, Lord.

Move the dullness out of the ear, Lord God. Cause our ears to hear thee. Bind the enemy, Lord, that would be in the midst to rob the word out of our hearts as soon as it is sown. Praise God, abase the old man, Lord God, crucify him that would rise up against you in rebellion, crucify him, Lord.

Render him (self) a death blow right now in the name of Jesus, the power of your sword this day. Cause our hearts to fear and tremble before thy mighty hand that we might be exalted by thee, O Lord, our God. Let thy word fall on good ground. Praise God in the highest. Let everything everywhere be subject unto you this day.

For thine is the authority, the power, and the kingdom. Praise your holy name forever and ever.

> *In those days came John the Baptist, preaching in the wilderness of Judæa, and saying, Repent ye: for the kingdom of heaven is at hand. For this is he that was spoken of by the prophet Esaias, saying,*
>
> *The voice of one crying in the wilderness, Prepare ye the way of the Lord, Make his paths straight.*
>
> *And the same John had his raiment of camel's hair, and a leathern girdle about his loins; and his meat was locusts and wild honey.*
>
> *Then went out to him Jerusalem, and all Judæa, and all the region round abut Jordan, and were baptized of him in Jordan, confessing their sins.*
>
> *But when he saw many of the Pharisees and Sadducees come to his baptism, he said unto them, O generation of vipers, who hath warned you to flee from the wrath to come?*
>
> *Bring forth therefore fruits meet for repentance: and think not to say within yourselves, We have Abraham to our father: for I say unto you, that God*

is able of these stones to raise up children unto Abraham.

And now also the axe is laid unto the root of the trees: therefore every tree which bringeth not forth good fruit is hewn down, and cast into the fire.

*I indeed baptize you with water unto repentance: but he that cometh after me is mightier than I, whose shoes I am not worthy to bear: he shall baptize you with the Holy Ghost,
and with fire: whose fan is in his hand, and he will throughly purge his floor, and gather his wheat into the garner; but he will burn up the chaff with unquenchable fire.*

Then cometh Jesus from Galilee to Jordan unto John, to be baptized of him. But John forbad him, saying, I have need to be baptized of thee, and comest thou to me? And Jesus answering said unto him, Suffer it to be so now: for thus it becometh us to fulfil all righteousness.

Then he suffered him. And Jesus, when he was baptized, went up straightway out of the water: and, lo, the heavens were opened unto him, and he saw the Spirit of God descending like a dove, and lighting upon him:

and lo a voice from heaven, saying, This is my beloved Son, in whom I am well pleased.

Praise God in the highest. The key verse here is number 15.

And Jesus answering said unto him, Suffer it to be so now: for thus it becometh us to fulfil all righteousness. Then he suffered him.

He allowed him to come into the water so that John may carry forth the complete work that God the Father sent him to do.

His job, John the Baptist, his job was to make straight the path of the Lord Jesus Christ. He was the forerunner of Jesus Christ, preparing the hearts by the preaching of the remission of sins, confessing of their sins, in order for Jesus to come and do that thorough work. It reminds me of the work of an evangelist and the work of an apostle. Amen.

Those two offices will tread in territories that others have not tread in order to prepare the hearts for the gospel of Jesus Christ and for the redemption of their souls. Amen.

And this is what John the Baptist did. He was the prophet of God, yet an evangelist, going about causing men and women to be stirred from their sleep and to awaken their eyes and their ears and their consciousness to know that they had need of redemption.

Many people everywhere need redemption, but not many know that they have need of redemption. And that's the difference. And that's why the preaching of the Word is given, that men might be awakened out of their sleep, that they might become aware of their true state of being in the eyes of God Almighty.

God sent Jesus Christ to reconcile mankind back unto Him, but first the truth must be heard, it must be declared, and it must be received and believed, and then acted upon before redemption can come into the life of an individual or individuals.

We must hear. If we do not hear, we cannot believe. And if we do not believe, we cannot receive. And if we do not reach out and receive by faith in Him, we cannot know Him. That's the way it is.

This is the ultimate plan of salvation. Praise God. And this is why the Word of God says, How can they hear without a preacher? And how can the preacher preach unless that preacher be sent by God? Many are going forth, and many are running without God. Because God has not commanded them, He has not ordained them, and therefore they cannot preach the whole counsel of God. They can only preach in part. See?

But the one that is sent of God will give you the gospel in its entirety. They'll see to it that you get the complete diet, the complete menu. It's offered. And then it's up to you, the individual, to take of that menu what you desire. But if you humble your heart, you will eat it all because God never sets before us anything that we have no need for.

Always remember that. What He offers unto us, we have need of it. Every day of our lives, what God offers to us of the Word of God, we have need of all of it. When He told the prophet Ezekiel, Eat ye all of it. Eat the whole scroll. Amen. He meant exactly that. Not what you want, Ezekiel, to tickle your heart. Word that I put within you, the scroll that you eat, it will be bitter in the mouth, but it will be sweet like honey in your stomach.

And that's the way the Word of God is. We may not always be up to the Word of God, but if we eat it, it's going to sweeten our very being. Praise God in the highest. So that's what you've got to do today, because the Word of God is going to find us where we should not be. And it's going to bring us where we ought to be if it's mixed with the faith of God in us. Amen.

So while I'm ministering the Word, ask God to give you faith to believe. Amen. We're going to speak about the humility of Jesus Christ.

Amen. Here, Jesus humbles himself, being the Lord Almighty, being the one sent from above. John was born of earthly parents, even though he was ordained of God in his mother Elizabeth's womb. Yet he was baptized with the Holy Ghost right in his mother's womb. And when Mary, the mother of Jesus, very pregnant with him, comes to tell her cousin Elizabeth all about the conception of Jesus Christ by the Holy Ghost in her womb, John, while he's yet in the womb, hears the salutation of Mary and his mother speaking with joy one to another and he himself was filled with the Holy Ghost while he's yet in the womb and leaps for joy knowing that the Lord from on high is already come but not born. Amen.

And we don't know, the Bible does not tell us anything more about John until he comes on the scene to make the path of Jesus straight in the hearts of the people. And you know how John did it? The first thing he said was, Repent! That was the first word of the gospel out of his mouth. Repent ye! For the kingdom of heaven is at hand.

And he knew it because he knew that Jesus was just a few months behind his birth. Amen. And those two did not grow up together. They did not grow up together. They did not have a chance to converse with one another.

God would not permit it to be. The prophet John was in the wilderness. He ate locusts and wild honey. That was his diet. Jesus grew up in his stepfather's carpentry shop. Amen. And he grew up in a natural setting of family life. In submission. Although he's the Lord from on high, he humbled himself to his earthly parents.

Mother Mary, stepfather Joseph. Showing us, every one of us, how we are to humble ourselves in submission to one another. Glory to God. Then, when it was time for Jesus to show forth the glory of God, his Father, in redeeming mankind back to God the Father. And bring in healing. Bring in salvation. Bring in restoration. Raise even the dead back to life. He allowed John to do his work first.

And at that precious appointed time, Jesus came on the scene. When John was about to go off the face of this earth, Jesus shows himself. And here John is telling everybody that there comes one mightier than he, whose shoes he was not able, not really worthy to bear.

And yet, when he saw Jesus coming, Jesus said, John, suffer me to be baptized. John said, No, I'm not worthy. And Jesus said, the scriptures must be fulfilled. And John submitted to the will of the Lord. John was taking the axe, the sword of God's mouth, telling those people, bringing down the strongholds of sin in their lives, bringing the hardness and impenitent heart, molding it just for Jesus, getting it just right for Jesus.

Whatever we want from God, there must be a preparation made in the heart. You just don't walk boldly in his presence and take him for granted. That's why we must ask, seek, and knock. We must show the Lord that we will humble ourselves, even as Christ our Lord.

Here is redemption coming from on high, and he humbles himself to a man that is born of the earth, that is begotten by a natural man, Zacharias and Elizabeth. Jesus humbles

222

himself to his cousin, but he's not looking at his cousin. He's looking at God, the Father's will.

God willed it so that Jesus be baptized, showing us that whatsoever Jesus did, we must do. Amen. That he brought glory and honor to the Father, and we, too, must humble ourselves and bring glory and honor to the Father.

Here he is, answering John back, John the Baptist, and saying, Suffer it to be sold now. God has an appointed time, and that was the appointed time for all that were gathered around the river of Jordan to see the Son of God baptized.

And God was just waiting for that chance to speak from heaven and say, This is my beloved Son in whom I am well pleased. It's amazing he never addressed John. Have you thought about that? John is in complete obedience to do the will of God, just like his cousin, Jesus Christ. But when God the Father speaks, he says, This is my beloved Son, and that is what makes the difference.

The Son is the one who draws us unto God the Father. It wasn't John who was doing the work of redemption in mankind's life. It was God the Father using John, but Jesus was to bring redemption, and that was the difference.

That's why the Father spoke and exalted his Son before all the earth that stood around the river of Jordan that day. And that's what we are here to do, to humble ourselves, not boast in our works, but bring glory and honor to the Father and lead everyone directly to Jesus Christ, the one who has redeemed us, who has given his life a ransom for us.

He did not do it for himself. He had no need to be redeemed, but he took upon himself, not just his shoulders, but upon his body as a whole, from the crown of his head to the soles of his feet. Jesus took upon himself our guilt that we might be redeemed from our sins, from our own guilt.

Now, I looked up the word submission. It's to yield to the power, control, or authority of another. It is to surrender. Subordinate means being dependent upon a greater authority... Being dependent upon a greater authority. Under the control or influence of someone else or something else. Submissiveness, or rather submissive, inclined to submit, to be obedient, humble.

And then the Holy Spirit just gave me this question. What is the difference between submission and commitment? Commit is to hand over for safekeeping. And this is what we do with our lives. We commit our lives to Jesus when we get saved. When we first come into the knowledge of salvation, we hand over our lives. We surrender it to him. We hand it over for safekeeping. And that's where we get the word saved. We're saved.

We're saved from self-destruction and from utter destruction. From being destroyed. We're saved from it. And only by committing our lives will we know him in the pardon of our sins. No matter how much we believe, there are many people out there that believe. Even the word of God says the devils believe, and they tremble. They tremble at what they know about God. See? But they're not committed.

And even if they were, God would not accept them because the judgment is already upon them. The judgment of God is already upon them. I was asked in prison last Sunday night, but won't God forgive satan? If he asked him, I said no.

And I think I shouted that with such venom against satan. But she jumped and she said, But he forgives us. I said yes.

You've got to remember that satan was created holy as Lucifer. But he's an enemy now. He's prone to do evil. And because of it, there is no place for redemption in his life. Jesus came to redeem man, not fallen spirits from on high. They're called the devil or demons.

But here we're to hand over for safekeeping our lives. That's commitment, to hand over for safekeeping, to deliver. Remember how Jesus offered up his body for everyone? He offered it up. He delivered it up, not just for us, but in obedience to the Father.

He submitted his will and his life to die because the Father had already commended it to be so. So every day that Jesus lived in a physical body, that ultimate thing was on his mind: to please the Father in all things. Small wonder, God the Father speaks from heaven while Jesus has been dipped in the River Jordan and being brought up by John the Baptist at that point.

Saying, This is my beloved son in whom I am well pleased. Now that's faith. That's the faith of God and faith in his son to carry out God's ultimate plan of redemption, all for mankind. The whole business of God in heaven is on the behalf of mankind on the earth, that he might bring glory to his name. And if anyone has a right to boast of who he is, it's God Almighty. He has every right because there's none like unto him.

He said, if there be any other God, I know none of. He said, I am the only God and beside me there is none other. Amen.

I am the creator. Praise God in the highest. So all the wood and all the hay and all the stubble and all the gold, all the silver and whatever, man will bow down in worship. God said, it's no God. It's no breath in it. If man bows down and worships the moon and the Sun and whatever, the stars and so forth, God says, I made that too.

I'm above it all. I am the greatest because I am the creator. Scientists have spent many, many years and many billions of dollars, trillions, I might say, to try to find out the glory of God through the elements, through the sun, through the moon, through the clouds, the rain, you name it.

And all they do is bring more glory and honor to God for what they find out, the wisdom and the knowledge that they find out. It brings glory to God because it's already written here. Already here.

And all they have to do is listen to a humble preacher, and they can save trillions of dollars. Many times, how long have we preached about the vices of man, bringing destruction to the body, to the lungs, and so forth? And man has spent millions and millions of dollars to test the fact out that this stuff will destroy the body.

All they had to do was listen to the humble preacher, and they would have been able to save many, many millions. And now they're writing warning, warning, but the preacher been out all along saying warning, warning, warning. Repent, and God will deliver you, and you don't have to be warned.

That's the whole duty of the preacher. He calls you to repent by preaching the gospel of repentance and bringing you into oneness with God and true fellowship. Amen.

Okay, commitment or committal is to involve yourself with God. Now this could be on any level with mankind, but we're speaking of God now, in whom we have to do. That's who we've got to answer to. This is how we've got to direct our lives daily. So maybe you might think on other things, but keep in mind the ultimate thing. We are to involve ourselves with God.

This is why Jesus came to bring us to that place that we might become involved totally, completely with God as his agents on earth. We are ambassadors, the Bible says, for Jesus Christ. Then he says we are to pledge.

We sing, what's his name, Bush. Had everybody pledging allegiance. Amen. And that is good. We are not to forget our nation. We thank God for our nation. We thank God for the freedom that we yet have in this nation. We thank God for it. Believe me, I thank God for it.

Every time I go out of this country and come back, honey, I thank God for it. I well know that this is not my final home. So I pledge allegiance to my father and to the kingdom of God. Amen. That's my first allegiance, to God.

When I was a little girl in school, I didn't know anyone else to pledge allegiance to but the flag and to the United States of America. But there's a greater country now, amen, that I am involved with. And this country, man did not make, man did not discover, it's from on high. Amen.

Glory to God in the highest. Then we entrust through commitment, we entrust our lives that we have turned over for safekeeping to God. Amen. Entrust is to give our lives in true faith and in confidence… and in confidence.

And that's where the struggle goes on. That's where it begins. The devil does not want us to have confidence in God. He wants us to start saying, But Lord, are you really able? If I really give myself over to you, will you really keep me? You just told me that in this world, I'm gonna have trouble. I don't think I'm willing to go through that. And then we'll start saying but, but, but, and the Lord is saying trust me, I cannot lie. I said I will keep you.

And one thing about him, he never strongholds us and binds us and overcomes us. It's all through our will that he'll woo us. Oh, he'll stay hard after us because he loves us, but he woos us, he draws us, he strives to get our attention.

And then he says whosoever will, that means in you, each individual, let them come. Now what is he doing? All the while he's standing, he's throwing out the power of God to give you that ability to come to him. But you've got to submit. You've got to become submissive to his will. You've got to entrust your life. You've got to turn it over to him.

You've got to take charge and say I give it to you of my free will. Freely I offer myself unto you. Just as you are, don't try to fix yourself up and then come. It'll never work. Just as you are, I don't care what condition you're in; if you're still mentally ill, come to Jesus.

That flicker of light which that mentally ill person may have…. Mentally ill person… that flicker of light, that's the moment that God has given you the power to think on his name. And when you think, you run.

That's what the Lord showed us Friday night. The name of the Lord is a strong tower; the righteous runneth into it. Don't you know it's right to believe God's Word? The moment that we get enlightenment in our hearts and minds, that's the moment to act upon God.

To act upon, to take him at his word. Praise God. And that's the conflict. The enemy will bring a conflict at that stage of our being. He'll start trying to pull you back, hold you back. After all, that's where God is bringing us from, it's from the devil's hands, from his dominion, from his power, from his authority.

That's why Jesus said, Behold, I give you power to become the sons of God, as many as believe on my name. We need that power. God's power. Always keep it in mind, God's power is the greatest. Not that it's greater, it's the greatest. There be no other power that can be greater than God's. Hallelujah.

The devil offers power to get the things of this world and tries to make you think that this is where it's at. But God gives us power to believe that this world has got to end. It's going to be burned. Everything's going up in smoke. So no matter what we obtain in this world, we are not to set our hearts upon it.

We are to bring glory to God for what he's brought to us in this world. We're to surrender it back to God and let him bless it that his kingdom might be built on this earth in the lives of the people. This is the only way God's kingdom is here is through the lives of his people.

And one day he's coming to take us out of here, that he might pour his wrath upon those that despise and hate him, that will not… have not surrendered to his authority. God means for us to submit ourselves unto his authority, to his power, to his keeping power.

Last Sunday, the Lord told us to seek the greatness of his power. And there be so many aspects of his power that it will take our entire days on the face of this earth that God has allowed unto us, or allotted unto us, to seek the greatness of his power.

So that means every day of our lives, he's going to be giving us greater enlightenment, greater revelation, greater understanding of the greatness of his power. And it cannot be exhausted.

Praise God in the highest. That's what I love about the word of God. Every time I go in it, there's some more to get, some more of his greatness to see. Hallelujah. And this is why my soul, like David, boasts in the Lord. This is why I'm always glorifying his name, because I see him greater and greater and greater.

And it's not that he becomes greater and greater; he cannot become any greater than he already is. It's that, unto us, He becomes greater, because we become more enlightened by the Spirit of God. The Holy Spirit is the one who shows us who he is.

Praise his holy name. Okay, let me finish with this. We are to commit with trust and confidence to the receiver. God receives us. He says, when we come to him, he will in no wise cast us out. In other words, he receives us.

And then the cleansing starts. The washing of our sins starts within us in actuality, even though it's already finished back at Calvary. But now, he's getting us one by one individually, and he's dealing with us according to our sins, according to our ways, according to our habits, according to our thoughts.

And he's got to take out, thoroughly wash, and put in. Take out, thoroughly wash, and put in. And this cycle goes on, and on, and on. And that's where we must submit ourselves daily. Mind you, I did not say commit. We must submit.

Every day of our lives, we must submit to the authority from on high if we are going to please him like Jesus did. Don't you want to hear the Father say, I love you, and I'm pleased with your life? The only way you'll hear that is by submitting unto God. Submitting every day.

And this is momentarily because the enemy ever watches, and he lingers to see a flaw in us. He studies our weaknesses. He studies our temperaments, our emotions. The enemy studies that. And anything that he can come to hit us with his daggers and his wicked inventions, he's going to do it. He's not afraid to try it.

He's not afraid. You ever have to keep that in mind. The devil is not afraid of us. He's afraid of God in us. Always keep that in mind, that God is the authority, and the devil fears and trembles at the authority of God.

But if we, the children of God, do not know how to exercise or execute the authority of God, the devil is going to take the advantage. This is why he came after Jesus in the wilderness. This is why he thought Jesus would be so weakened through fasting and praying, so weakened in spirit and weakened in body. This is the ultimate time to get him.

So when Jesus ended the fast, this is immediately after he was baptized by John, he was led of the Spirit of God into the wilderness to be tempted of the devil. Can you imagine the Holy Ghost that had just baptized him? After he came up out of the water from the baptism of water, the Holy Ghost descended upon him as a dove in the likeness of a dove, and then immediately, straightway, the Bible says, he led him into the wilderness.

The Holy Spirit led him there so that he may know the struggles that we go through. He's out there, isolated in the physical being, all alone with devils. Every temptation that is named under the sun, Jesus encountered out there in the wilderness, fasting. And so now the fast is ended, and there's no food in the wilderness.

So Jesus begins to come out of the wilderness. The devil knows. He's watching him, watching him all along. Now, all his demons have done their job, and now they can't go any further, so satan himself comes on the scene. And he says, if thou be the Son of God, turn these stones into bread. He's coming at Jesus where he knows he's the weakest.

Jesus desires to eat. The body needs food. But Jesus turns on him with the power of the sword. It is written. It is written. And dear ones, unless you become like Jesus and say it is written, you can bind the blood on satan all you want to. You can say, Get behind me, devil, all you want to. But unless you come at the devil with the sword, the sword of God, the mighty sword is the word of God written, but alive in our hearts as we eat it daily, as we 'eat it daily.

Jesus is the Word. So he knew how to come after him. And Jesus said, It is written. Man shall not live by bread alone...alone. Knowing that we needed the bread, but that's not what keeps us alive. But by every word that proceeds out of the mouth of God shall man live. See? This is what keeps us alive. satan comes to buffet our minds.

He came to buffet Jesus at his weakest point, but Jesus stood faithful. And this is where we have got to get integrity in Christ. We've got to get holy zeal in Christ.

We must stand up with zeal. I don't care how feeble we are or how worn we are. The Holy Spirit that was enabling Jesus to stand the test is the same Spirit of God on the scene today in our lives, enabling us, if we so desire, to stand the test of temptation. Amen.

This is why we Christians went berserk when this movie came out. And we heard that it was coming out because we knew that it was an injustice to the word of God. And bring in another kind of gospel that has not been recorded here. Man is trying to make...well, satan, through man, is trying to make Jesus look like he was nothing but a human being. But the devil is a liar.

He's a liar. Jesus said he's the father of lies. Jesus said that they would blaspheme him. And they would blaspheme the father, they would blaspheme the son. But whosoever blasphemeth the Holy Ghost shall not be forgiven. So that movie maker is treading on dangerous grounds. Dangerous grounds because the Holy Ghost has set on record who Jesus is.

And any man take away or add thereto, watch out, because the plagues of this book, the curses of God, be upon them. Now, this is how dangerous that man stands. God knows the one that rephrased the Living Bible has lost his voice and shaken like an old man, too old beyond his years, because he dared to take upon himself to change the word of God that people full of sin might understand the word. No natural man can understand the word of God. It's spiritually discerned.

We must be dependent upon the Holy Ghost at all times to reveal the mysteries of the kingdom of heaven unto us. If we try to break it down to our feeble understanding, we're going to rob God of his glory. The Holy Spirit is here to give us understanding, but the person that do not want to submit his will to God, well, the Holy Ghost will not enlighten them. See?

So that calls for responsibility on our part. We must be responsible unto God by yielding, and this is another word, yielding to God, giving up to him.

Have you ever been on the highway, you who are drivers, when you drive, you come to a merging in the road, and you'll see the word merge or yield. Yield means to give the right away to, and that's what we do. We yield our members unto God, and we give the right of way to God in our lives every day. Yielding can be, yield not to temptation, as the song says, but we don't want to yield to temptation.

The true child of God does not want to yield. It's not in our hearts to yield, yet God requires us to yield to him. Our hearts, thoughts may be in us that are pure, desires may be in us that are pure, but it may not be the perfect will of God for us at that appointed time. So what do we do? We yield the right of way to God. He has the right to direct our feet in the path that he has ordained. See, I'm reminded of Paul.

Paul proposed to go to Asia. Then, a great missionary, a great evangelist, he's purposing to go into Asia, and the Holy Spirit speaks and says, Paul, do not go into Asia at this time. Now, there was nothing wrong with Paul desiring to go into Asia to present the gospel of Jesus, to win the souls of the needy that sat in darkness. There was nothing wrong with that. That was what he was commended to do:

to go to the Gentiles. He was an apostle to the Gentiles, and he knew that he had not covered Asia at that point, so he purposed in his heart to head for Asia.

And the Holy Ghost said, Paul, go not into Asia at this time. And Paul had to yield the right of way in submission to the will of God because God knows every aspect of our lives. He knows when it's the right time, and he knows when there's a timing of wrong. No doubt, Paul would have been killed long before his time had he gone into Asia, but he yielded to the voice of the Holy Ghost.

I pray that you search your hearts as God is bringing this word today, because many times, as Christians, we take our own lives in our hands, and we direct our footsteps instead of God. Therefore, he is not Lord in our lives when we are in that condition.

We are still lords of our lives. And the Bible says that there's only one Lord, one faith, and one baptism. So if we are lords of our own lives, then Christ is not ruling.

And if Christ is not ruling, then we are not indeed the sons of God, because if we are the sons of God, we are yielded in obedience and humble submission to God at all times. Our ear is ever waiting to hear him. Our heart is ever longing to be directed from his word. Amen and amen.

This is why the spirit of prophecy is given. This is why God speaks in prophecy to his church. The gifts of the Holy Ghost, the spirit of wisdom and knowledge, amen, of discerning of spirits. The Holy Spirit will put in one to discern what's going on inside of another. And then you're moved by the power of prophecy to speak to that individual or to speak to that body of believers, to give us guidance, to give us direction, to let us know what's on his mind.

And this is most important. God doesn't want us to walk around like zombies and spineless and mindless. That's not his will for us.

We're to show forth the intelligence of God. And the only way we can is we've got to walk close with him and be yielded in humble submission, to be instructed, to be governed, and to allow the Holy Spirit to work in us continually. We're ever learning who he is.

Let us not be of those that Paul warned of, ever learning and never coming to the knowledge of the truth, and who is the truth but Jesus. We want to know him. Sunday school department, get to know who Jesus is. This is why you're not free in your spirit to praise him because you have not met him. When you meet him, you've got nothing but praise for him. Glory to his name.

I love Rochelle's testimony when she found out who he is. She didn't know, and bitterness and all of this was in her heart because she didn't know him, and she didn't want to turn her life over to somebody that maybe it might be a mistake, perhaps not true at all. So she set out in her heart, no matter what went on in her mind, no matter how the enemy buffeted her, she wanted to know, does he really exist? And I can identify with that testimony.

I wanted to know, do you really exist? Like I have been taught. John the Baptist had suffered and been cast in prison after all that mighty work of preparation for Jesus Christ, and then God's not answering it seems. Jesus won't come to visit him, and he's hearing nothing, no encouragement, and his own disciples are out of work and so he said to one of his disciples, Go… go and ask Jesus if he'd be the one or do we look for another? Isn't that like us in our weakest point? Jesus, did you forget? Are you gonna keep your word? Are you really telling the truth? Jesus said, Go and tell John the mighty works you see me doing.

They went back and they told John what Jesus was doing. Jesus never said, Tell him to be of good courage. I'll be over to see him tomorrow. As soon as I'm finished here, I'll get him out of prison. Jesus knew that John's time was up, and when he sent his disciples, John's disciples back with the report of all the work that Jesus was doing, Jesus turned to the people and said, What went you out for to see?

He started bragging about John, but John didn't hear it. John is behind closed doors in the dungeon, getting ready to get his head chopped off. And when John's disciples went back, telling of the mighty works of Jesus. John said He must increase, I must decrease. John submitted himself to death; John knew he was as good as dead. When Jesus didn't come but sent the word back of the mighty acts of God, John Knew...

THE MIGHTY WORKS OF JESUS

First Aired April 30th, 1995

God is good to us. Praise his holy name. We just thank the Lord for your prayers.

Father God, in the authority of Jesus' name, we thank you for this glorious day in which you've made for us to enter therein. In this, we give thanks, O Lord, forever and ever. Thy word, Lord God, is a lamp unto our feet and a light unto our pathway. It is you, Lord, who leads us and guides us in the way that you would have us to go.

And as we go into the fifth chapter of St. Matthew, enlighten our eyes and open our ears and melt our hearts that we might see and hear and be satisfied with thy sure word. Glory be to God in the highest. Have your mighty way today. Let the anointing of the Holy Spirit have preeminence over the word of God and over the vessels that you've called unto honor to bring glory and praise, and honor to your name. Have your mighty way today. Thy will be done, thy kingdom come in the greatness of your power, Father.

We ask it in the all-powerful, almighty, authoritative name of Jesus, the name that is above every name. Glory be to God. We thank you for the power that's in the name of Jesus, for deliverance that's in the name of Jesus, for victory that comes only through the name of Jesus.

Thy word be accomplished for that which you send it to do, thy will be done.

The first verse of Matthew 5,

> *And seeing the multitudes, he went up into a mountain: and when he was set, his disciples came unto him: and he opened his mouth, and taught them, saying,*
>
> *Blessed are the poor in spirit: for their's is the kingdom of heaven.*
>
> *Blessed are they that mourn: for they shall be comforted.*
>
> *Blessed are the meek: for they shall inherit the earth.*
>
> *Blessed are they which do hunger and thirst after righteousness: for they shall be filled.*
>
> *Blessed are the merciful: for they shall obtain mercy.*
>
> *Blessed are the pure in heart: for they shall see God.*
>
> *Blessed are the peacemakers: for they shall be called the children of God.*
>
> *Blessed are they which are persecuted for righteousness' sake: for their's is the kingdom of heaven.*
>
> *Blessed are ye, when men shall revile you, and persecute you, and shall say all manner of evil against you falsely, for my sake. Rejoice, and be exceeding glad: for great is your reward in heaven:*

Let me repeat that.

> *Rejoice, and be exceeding glad: for great is your reward in heaven: for so persecuted they the prophets which were before you.*
>
> *Ye are the salt of the earth: but if the salt have lost his savour, wherewith shall it be salted? it is thenceforth good for nothing, but to be cast out, and to be trodden under foot of men.*
>
> *Ye are the light of the world. A city that is set on an hill cannot be hid. Neither do men light a candle, and put it under a bushel, but on a candlestick; and it giveth light unto all that are in the house.*
>
> *Let your light so shine before men, that they may see your good works, and glorify your Father which is in heaven.*
>
> *Think not that I am come to destroy the law, or the prophets: I am not come to destroy, but to fulfil. For verily I say unto you, Till heaven and earth pass, one jot or one tittle shall in no wise pass from the law, till all be fulfilled.*
>
> *Whosoever therefore shall break one of these least commandments, and shall teach men so, he shall be called the least in the kingdom of heaven: but whosoever shall do and teach them, the same shall be called great in the kingdom of heaven. For I say unto you, That except your righteousness shall exceed the righteousness of the scribes and Pharisees, ye shall in no case enter into the kingdom of heaven.*

Ye have heard that it was said by them of old time,
Thou shalt not kill; and whosoever shall kill shall
be in danger of the judgment: but I say unto you,
That whosoever is angry with his brother without a
cause shall be in danger of the judgment: and
whosoever shall say to his brother, Raca, shall be in
danger of the council: but whosoever shall say,
Thou fool, shall be in danger of hell fire.

Therefore if thou bring thy gift to the altar, and
there rememberest that thy brother hath ought
against thee; leave there thy gift before the altar,
and go thy way; first be reconciled to thy brother,
and then come and offer thy gift.

Agree with thine adversary quickly, whiles thou art
in the way with him; lest at any time the adversary
deliver thee to the judge, and the judge deliver thee
to the officer, and thou be cast into prison. Verily I
say unto thee, Thou shalt by no means come out
thence, till thou hast paid the uttermost farthing.

Ye have heard that it was said by them of old time,
Thou shalt not commit adultery: but I say unto you,
That whosoever looketh on a woman to lust after
her hath committed adultery with her already in his
heart.

And if thy right eye offend thee, pluck it out, and
cast it from thee: for it is profitable for thee that one
of thy members should perish, and not that thy
whole body should be cast into hell. And if thy right
hand offend thee, cut it off, and cast it from thee: for
it is profitable for thee that one of thy members
should perish, and not that thy whole body should

be cast into hell. It hath been said, Whosoever shall put away his wife, let him give her a writing of divorcement: but I say unto you, That whosoever shall put away his wife, saving for the cause of fornication, causeth her to commit adultery: and whosoever shall marry her that is divorced committeth adultery.

Again, ye have heard that it hath been said by them of old time, Thou shalt not forswear thyself, but shalt perform unto the Lord thine oaths: but I say unto you, Swear not at all; neither by heaven; for it is God's throne:

Let me repeat that, verse 34.

but I say unto you, Swear not at all; neither by heaven; for it is God's throne: nor by the earth; for it is his footstool: neither by Jerusalem; for it is the city of the great King.

Neither shalt thou swear by thy head, because thou canst not make one hair white or black. But let your communication be, Yea, yea; Nay, nay: for whatsoever is more than these cometh of evil.

Ye have heard that it hath been said, An eye for an eye, and a tooth for a tooth: but I say unto you, That ye resist not evil: but whosoever shall smite thee on thy right cheek, turn to him the other also.

And if any man will sue thee at the law, and take away thy coat, let him have thy cloke also. And whosoever shall compel thee to go a mile, go with him twain.

Give to him that asketh thee, and from him that would borrow of thee turn not thou away.

Ye have heard that it hath been said, Thou shalt love thy neighbour, and hate thine enemy. But I say unto you, Love your enemies, bless them that curse you, do good to them that hate you, and pray for them which despitefully use you, and persecute you; that ye may be the children of your Father which is in heaven: for he maketh his sun to rise on the evil and on the good, and sendeth rain on the just and on the unjust.

For if ye love them which love you, what reward have ye? do not even the publicans the same? And if ye salute your brethren only, what do ye more than others? do not even the publicans so? Be ye therefore perfect, even as your Father which is in heaven is perfect.

Now we're living in a day of apostasy, where the Word of God is not believed as it is written. Men are trying to turn God's Word to suit themselves. Men are going by philosophies. Many are leading people astray because of their own doctrines.

Jesus said he did not come to destroy the law or the prophets. Jesus is the fulfillment of the law. So what was said in the law, Jesus came, being the grace and the mercies of God, manifesting God's loving-kindness, God's forgiveness, God's way of life. Jesus lived the way of the Father before the sons of men. This is why we know Jesus to be the door to heaven.

We have read and you have heard how Jesus said here in the fifth chapter of Saint Matthew, it has been said. He states that several times. But immediately following, Jesus says, But I say unto you.

He's giving us a more clear way, a more righteous way, a perfect way to live. And at the end of the chapter, he says, Be ye therefore perfect, verse 48, even as your Father which in heaven is perfect. And we hear people say, Well, you can't live perfect, but we can obey.

Obedience brings perfection. If we obey God's Word, we will be pleasing in the eyes of God. And that's what God is talking about, perfection. To be pleasing before God. And we should strive for the testimony of Jesus. Thou art my beloved Son in whom I am well-pleased.

The same Jesus that we say is our Savior, and we say that he is our Lord. We say that he is our friend. We say that we are following him. Well, this same Jesus walked by the leading of the Holy Ghost. And the Holy Ghost empowered Jesus in the hours of temptation to be strong, to be an overcomer. The Word of God says, Jesus learned obedience to the things that he suffered.

And Jesus set that perfect example for us. Be ye perfect, even as your Father in heaven is perfect. What God requires of us, he's already made provisions for us to be victorious in it. He's given us Jesus to forgive us, to take the place on Calvary where we should have been. Remember the two, one on each side of Jesus as Jesus hung dying? He made his death, his grave, amongst the sinners. He hung there between two sinners.

Remember, they were being crucified too for their deeds. And while Jesus hung dying, one asked him to remember him when he goes into his kingdom. And Jesus said, This day shall thou be with me in paradise. Jesus forgave the sinner who was hanging there dying for his guilt. Jesus took that sinner's guilt on that side of him upon himself. And he was also taking the other's guilt.

But the other rejected him. He didn't care for Jesus to pay the price for him. He called himself, rebuking him, mocking the Lord who had come for him. Jesus knows the way that we take. Every one of us was doomed to die for our sins and be eternally separated from God, but God sent Jesus to redeem us from our carelessness, from our wickedness, from our cold-heartedness, from our indifference, from our rebellion, from every evil thought, from every evil way, from every evil lust. God sent Jesus to deliver us.

So if Jesus did all of this for us and the power of the Holy Ghost enabled him to go through, being strengthened by the angelic host that came to him to minister strength to go through for our sakes, should not God require that we obey him? If Jesus took our place, it is only just and right for God to require us to obey him. We couldn't go to the cross for ourselves. God needed one that was spotless, and everyone was guilty.

Jesus is the only one who was spotless before God Almighty, and Jesus told us to be of good cheer. What a mighty big brother taking our place. Amen. A big brother, a good and mighty brother, a friend… our Jesus.

So God is telling us right here in the fifth chapter of St. Matthew how we're to be in spirit, how we're to be in our minds, how we're to live in our hearts before God. He's talking to his own now.

The world cannot receive this. When the Lord tells us to turn the other cheek, the carnal mind or the worldly mind will say, No way. I'll get them before they get me.

I'm no sissy. I'm gonna stand up for myself. Nobody else is going to do it, but Jesus said Turn the other cheek. That's not a dummy. That's one that's given a battle over to God, and God knows how to fight for you. God knows how to avenge you.

Amen. God will take you into his captivity, and God will defend you on every side. So it takes strength to turn the battle to God and not to retaliate in your own mind and your own ways. Amen. It's better to let God do the fighting. God, the Word of God, says, will take vengeance. Vengeance belongs to God. Hallelujah.

The Lord tells us that we are to be merciful, and you know how easily we can do that? We think of ourselves. How we want someone to show us mercy. If we have any sense whatsoever, we would put ourselves in that person's place and we think soberly. Lord, if that was me, I'd want someone to show me mercy.

So before they even ask, I ask your mercy upon them. God loves that and God remembers that. He remembers our actions. God remembers our thoughts. God remembers these things. Either they are against us or they're for us, the thoughts of God. You know why? Because God recompenses. God rewards us for the good that we do.

God rewards us for the evil that we do. This is why the Lord Jesus said, Blessed are they. And we see it 1, 2, 3, 4, 5, 6, 7, 8 times. Amen.

Blessed are they that are poor in spirit. Blessed are they that mourn. Blessed are they, blessed are the meek. Blessed are they which do hunger and thirst after righteousness. Blessed are the merciful. Blessed are the pure in heart. Blessed are the peacemakers. Blessed are they which are persecuted for righteousness' sake. Blessed are ye when men shall revile you and persecute you and shall slay all manner of evil against you falsely for my sake. Amen.

But every time he would say Blessed are they, he has something added... a glorious blessing. When he says blessed are the poor in spirit, here's the blessing. For theirs is the kingdom of heaven. Blessed are they that mourn. Here's the blessing. For they shall be comforted. Oh, no one can comfort you like God. No one can comfort you like the Most High.

He says Blessed are the meek. He didn't say the weak. The meek. The lowly in heart that chooses the way of the Lord Most High. He said Blessed are the meek, for they shall inherit the earth, not as the earth is today. Glory be to God. But when Jesus comes to rule on the earth, it's our inheritance.

For where Jesus is, it's heaven. Amen. Glory to God in the highest. He says Blessed are the merciful, for they shall obtain mercy and bless the Lord. We need God's mercy. Amen.

In our transactions and business, we need the mercies of God. I see men that they'll go out of their way to try to get men to accept them, and that they might be pleased and get favors from men. Some will sell their souls just to be favorable in the eyes of men. But all you have to do is please God. Be merciful in your own hearts, and God will show you mercy. God never forgets.

Hallelujah. Don't you ever think that God is like man. Man, you will do good favors towards them, and they will go on.

They receive those favors, and they go on their way and forget most of them. But not God. God will reward us and not in the time when Jesus comes for us only but in this present world. God will reward us. We desire to go God's way. Hallelujah.

But Jesus tells us that when we are persecuted for righteousness' sake, he tells us to rejoice and be exceeding glad. That was one most valuable lesson I had to learn. We should rejoice when our names are out there as evil, and when men will reject us for the love of God that's in our hearts. Amen.

When they will say all manner of evil against us falsely for Jesus' sake, for the way of the Lord, because we have chosen to walk the way of God. You see, it's our choice to walk God's way. Hallelujah. The Lord tells us to rejoice and be exceeding glad. It's a marvelous thing to do. That means you're dead to your self-life. When you can rejoice through the things that you suffer for Jesus' sake, you've ceased from this world, you've ceased from sin.

Praise God in the highest. That is one glorious victory to have. To be able to rejoice and be exceeding glad and say, Lord, I praise you anyhow. Hallelujah. I live for you anyhow. No matter what has been said against me, no matter how greatly I'm hated, I love you and I'll please you anyhow… You've got all heaven on your side.

He says, You're the salt of the earth, but if the salt has lost its savor, if the salt has lost its strength. He asked the question, Wherewith shall it be salted? You sit down before a meal, and it needs salt. Amen. Nothing tastes as good as a meal with salt. You sit down, and there's no salt in that food.

No matter how appetizing it may look, it is not good to the palate. It takes the salt to make it taste as it should taste. And that's what the Lord is saying about us. Amen. We're in this world and we'll salt it with salt. Amen. But if the salt has lost its strength, if it has lost its savor, it's no good. It doesn't taste good. We're not pleasing to God.

When we say with the psalmist, Oh, taste and see that the Lord is good. Don't you think God is testing us out also? Amen. To see if his goodness is abiding in us. He puts us through. God tries the rains of the heart. Yes, he does.

And he means for us to be salted. So persecution brings salt. Glory be to God. That's what God is looking for. Who can stand in the hour of tribulation and persecution? That's the one that's going to make it all the way through if they keep their eyes on the Lord.

Many have gone through persecution, but they have gotten weary, and they've thrown up their hands. Can't take it anymore. And they start fighting back in the flesh. They've lost their strength. They've lost their savor. And men can take that backslider in heart and do anything they want to. That's what he's saying here.

Wherewith shall it be salted is then swapped good for nothing, but to be cast out and to be trodden underfoot of men. But God will not let men walk over those that are salted for the kingdom of God's sake. He won't do it.

And look what he says about those that are salted. You're the light of the world. A city that is set on a hill cannot be hid. So don't try to hide your testimony. Amen. We're to be shining as beacon lights in this darkened world. And what a glorious time to be alive. I mean, it's a marvelous time to shine brightly for the Lord because darkness is all around us.

Men have forgotten to walk the right way. They don't know anymore. This younger generation is not a generation of churchgoers. Their parents have left off following the Lord God of hosts. And their children are coming up without God or without any knowledge of God. So all they're taught is in a humanistic manner.

They're taught to love themselves, and to feast upon the desires and the lust of the flesh and the eyes and the pride of this life. They have made themselves gods to their own destruction. And this is in our time, that we are living in now.

Many have failed God. And this is why we have the generation that we have today. Darkness, blindness, ignorant of God, ignorant of God's will, ignorant of the purpose and plan that God has set for their lives.

So we have to shine his lights to them. We have to shine brightly unto them. And don't think just because many are abiding in darkness that they don't want God. It's a lot of people out there who will come to this light if we shine for Jesus. Hallelujah. There are many out there that have not known that God loves them, that God has sent his son for their own good.

Even in this hour, when we see heathenistic manners on every side. God has a people that have yet not known who

Jesus is. And this is why we must shine. We must allow Jesus to shine through us, and we must wholeheartedly follow Jesus so that that glorious light may be a beacon to those who are in darkness. Don't be ashamed of Jesus Christ. Don't be ashamed of his sufferings and of his dying because Jesus is alive.

He rose from the dead. Glory be to God. He triumphed over death, hell, and the grave. He's that glorious light. Amen. That's shining even now from on high through us. Glory to God in the highest. Let us declare that which we know unto those that are abiding in darkness. I don't go along with that idea that I don't have to be a witness with my mouth.

Yes, we witness with our lives, but we witness also to that which God has done in our lives. God didn't save us to be mum. But, however you follow Jesus through the word, whenever Jesus wrought deliverance, there was confession of who God is.

Remember the man who was blind all his life? Amen. And Jesus healed him. The man received his sight. And his parents... they were glad that he could see, and they acknowledged that that was their son. But as far as who did it, ask him. In other words, they didn't want to be cast out of the synagogue.

They wanted to stay right there amongst those that had been in church with, all their lives. But the one that had received his sight, whether mama or daddy, confessed Jesus Christ or not. He told them in the synagogue that Jesus did it. Now, at first, he was not sure himself. But Jesus let him know that he was the one who brought deliverance to him, and he went back and he told them that the Lord Jesus opened his eyes.

And the rulers of the synagogue didn't want the blind the former blind man to tell others that Jesus did it. And God used the former blind man on the Pharisees. Witnessing Christ Jesus, that he's a good man. A powerful man.

Glory to God in the highest. And we're to open our mouths wide and let the Lord be seen. Let your light, Jesus is the light of the world, let your light so shine. Glory to God in the highest. He said Let your light so shine before men that they may see your good works and glorify your father which is in heaven. What works? The works of righteousness. Amen.

> *Think not that I am come to destroy the law, or the prophets: I am not come to destroy, but to fulfil. For verily I say unto you, Till heaven and earth pass, one jot or one tittle shall in no wise pass from the law, till all be fulfilled.*

And Jesus is that fulfillment. Whatever God says thou shalt not do, when you receive Jesus, you will not do. Amen. Whatever God has said of old that he is against, when we receive Jesus, we are also against. Amen. It's the love that God puts in our hearts, and it's the seed of righteousness that God plants there.

Jesus is the righteousness of God. And when we receive him, righteousness is planted in us, and it grows. Hallelujah. And every day that we walk with Jesus and every day that we read of him and sup with him, we grow in the righteousness of God. Hallelujah.

So we fulfill, amen, everything that God is after, everything that God said thou shalt not do. We fulfill the purpose of God by following Jesus. That's how we please God. That's how we are made perfect in heart. Blessed are the pure in heart, for they shall see God. They shall see God. It's the pure; it's those who are striving to please him. Amen. And striving, God enables us by his power to overcome.

That's why you say strive to enter in at the straight gate. Hallelujah. It's good to live on Straight Street before the straight gate. Praise God in the highest.

And Jesus said, except our righteousness is seed the righteousness of the Scribes and Pharisees, we shall in no wise enter into the kingdom of heaven. We have to do more than those who say thou shalt not. Amen. We have to be doers of that, which Jesus requires.

And the glorious fact is that God is not telling us to do this of ourselves. We cannot, that's why Jesus had to come. But we put on the Lord Jesus Christ. And we choose every day of our lives to follow Jesus. And that's how we become well-pleasing in the Father's sight. This is how we bring glory. This is how we glorify the Father: is following Jesus. He tells us not to kill. When we have received him, there is no desire to kill.

When we're following in the spirit of the Most High God, we don't want to hurt anyone. When we're in the carnal, that's the Christian who is walking earthward. Or when the sinner has not known God, we're subject to anything. Because God is not ruling. He's not holding the reins of the heart.

But to follow him, there is no desire to harm or inflict a wound on anyone. We see that vessel as God sees them. Most precious in God's sight. Amen. When we're in the flesh, we're subject to anything. The Word of God says,

*But I say unto you, That whosoever is angry with
his brother without a cause shall be in danger of the
judgment:*

And we don't use that word fool so easily either. When you
say to a person…when you call a person a fool, you're
saying a mighty word. They are void of understanding.
They are void of the righteousness of God.

That fool is in danger of hellfire themselves. Because the
Word of God says a fool has said in his heart, there is no
God. So you can't use that word lightly.

When you say you are a fool. You'd better say it through
the wisdom and the knowledge of God because God does
not take it lightly when you call a person a fool. Amen.

Now the Word of God says you fools and you're blind.
That's a person who has no desire to come after God. That's
the fool. Amen. Blind in heart because only God gives
sight.

Now, the right thing to do in God's eyes is when one has an
ought against you, the Holy Spirit will make that thing
known, and many times he doesn't have to; we already
know. The Lord said Leave your gift at the altar and go be
reconciled. Get it right, be at peace with one another. Strive
for peace. Seek peace and pursue it. Amen.

They don't want peace at that moment, wait a little while,
pray some more. Go back again, strive for peace because
God is a God of peace. The Word of God says he's not the
author of confusion but a God of peace. Amen. Many
times, a person will not let you make peace with them, but
in your heart, you know, you've done the right thing,
striving for peace. Amen.

255

If that person wants to remain at odds, don't you be at odds. You'd be ready at any time that person changed their attitude towards you. You be ready to forgive, ready to receive. Amen. That's the way of the Lord, and his way is right.

Praise His Holy Name. If we would practice this, the world would be far greater. Far greater. The devil wants confusion. He wants division. He wants to bring a wide gap between mankind. But Jesus is the author of peace. The Word of God says he is the Prince of Peace. Now, we must walk in his wisdom.

Like I said, many will not want peace. The Word of God tells us how in their heart they'll say one thing with their mouth, they'll say peace with their mouth, but in their heart, they lie and wait for you.

So you have to walk in wisdom. Remember David in King Saul's home? David had to walk in wisdom. He knew Saul wanted to kill him, but David sought peace in spite of it. Amen. And David had to run for his life. Many times, he was on the run because the King, old King Saul, ruled by jealousy, wanted to destroy David, who was already anointed to take his place. But David prevailed because he sought peace. Amen.

And that's the way we must live. People will not speak to one another. And the Lord tells us to speak to our enemies. Let your righteousness exceed the righteousness of the scribes and Pharisees. Many times, I'm put on the front line that way. Amen.

People act like you're a heathen, they act like you're some vicious animal. They'll look the other way. They'll even cross the street and go another way to keep from looking at you, to speak to you. But the Lord says, salute them when you come in the way with them. Salute them. God grants the opportunity, speak to them.

Don't act like they are not there. If you act like them, the Lord says you're no better than the scribe or the Pharisee. And if you're no better than they, you're not entering God's kingdom.

But speak to those who hate you. You treat them just like you're their best friend when you come into their presence. That's the best way to defeat the devil in them. Hallelujah. You show forth the love of God. You'll be that burning light. Hallelujah. It's the way of the Lord. And his way is right. Bless his holy name. Now in verse 31,

> *It hath been said, Whosoever shall put away his wife, let him give her a writing of divorcement:*

Mm-hmm. Moses only allowed it because man's heart was already doing it. And Moses was trying to keep order. So Moses, because of the hardness of their hearts, wrote that precept. Jesus said, but Jesus also said from the beginning it was not so. From the beginning, God did not ordain it, divorcement. Amen. But here's what Jesus said,

> *but I say unto you, That whosoever shall put away his wife, saving for the cause of fornication,*

Uh-huh, you see, there is a clause. You can get a divorce. That's what man is saying…fornication is not adultery. Fornication is sexual intercourse between single people… Fornication. Amen. If you're married and one commits adultery, that's still having sexual intercourse outside of marriage. With another person and they're already married to their wife or to their husband, God says forgive them. Forgive them.

But man, it's just like of old, they will not forgive. They say this is a clause for divorcement. You say, well then, why did Jesus say that? Remember Mary and Joseph when they were betrothed to one another? We call it in our day, in the Western world, engaged. They had given themselves to one another to be married in the very future. And Mary found herself with child.

Found herself carrying Jesus, Jesus being planted in her womb while she's still single by the Holy Ghost. And Joseph thought Mary had committed fornication against him. So Joseph purposed in his heart that he would secretly, quietly put her away.

He loved her, and he didn't want to bring shame upon her. So he was going to quietly put her away because of fornication, he thought. This is his desire, but the angel of the Lord appeared unto Joseph in a dream and told Joseph, Fear not to take Mary unto thyself to be your wife. So Joseph married Mary following the angel's instruction. Amen.

He married her while she was pregnant with Jesus Christ. And that's what Jesus means by saving for the cause of fornication, or except it be for the reason of fornication. Amen. To be betrothed or engaged is just as sacred. You have made a vow between you two. And it's just as sacred as the marriage vow, also in the eyes of God.

Because you have given yourself by vow to that individual until you come into the marriage itself. Amen. That's how God looks at things. God sees things altogether different than the children of men. This is why we always have to be seeking after the mind of the Most High. And here plainly Jesus states,

> *but I say unto you,*

verse 32,

> *That whosoever shall put away his wife,*

And it is called just that when you're engaged to an individual, that's your intended wife, that's your intended husband.

> *saving for the cause of fornication, causeth her to commit adultery: and whosoever shall marry her that is divorced committeth adultery.*

Now remember verse 19?

> *Whosoever therefore shall break one of these least commandments, and shall teach men so, he shall be called the least in the kingdom of heaven: but whosoever shall do and teach them, the same shall be called great in the kingdom of heaven.*

Many preachers are going to lose their reward because they are teaching people that it's all right to get divorced. Amen. And God does not want man to be alone, go and get another wife.

But Jesus said, and whosoever marrieth her that is divorced committed adultery. It is so plain that a fool could not err, Jesus said. I wrestled with this all night and all day because I was wanting to get a divorce, and God took his word… and every argument that self could come up with, God would take his word and show me God's better way. Amen.

And this is why the apostle Paul says, If the unbelieving depart, let them depart. Don't try to keep them there, bound in a marriage that they do not want any part of. Let them have their liberty, let them go on their way. He said, A brother or sister is not in bondage to such things, but let them remain… Let them remain true to God, true to their marriage vow.

Don't seek a divorce. Oh, I'm going to be called great in God's kingdom. You see how God weighs greatness.

If I were a well-known evangelist, all over the world, men would call me great. She's got power with God… God is using her mightily, but because I teach this, I'm rejected. I'm persecuted. But here's what Jesus said, whosoever shall do and teach them, do it first. So I've done it. I'm yet doing it. Amen.

He says the same shall be called great in the kingdom of God or the kingdom of heaven. That's the way of the Lord. And so be it, so be it. Let God's word be true in every man, a liar that is contrary to God's word. They are a liar. Hallelujah. Children would be better off mentally, emotionally, and physically if people would do it God's way. Hallelujah.

Let's do what Jesus says unto us. What did the father say to Peter when Jesus was transformed and he was conversing with Elijah and Moses? Hallelujah. This is my beloved son, Hear ye him. Listen to him… My beloved, He's the one that I sent from heaven. You hear him. Moses went to heaven and Elijah went to heaven, but I sent Jesus from heaven, Amen. You hear him, glory to God in the highest.

Jesus is the fulfillment of the Mosaic law, of the prophets. What they preach, what they proclaim, Jesus fulfilled.

When we follow Jesus, we're pleasing God. So let us hear, let us obey, let us do the will of God.

> *Be ye therefore perfect, even as your Father which is in heaven is perfect.*

Let us grow in his grace. Let us grow in the knowledge of Jesus Christ. Let us grow in the ways of the most high God, and let us be doers of the word and fellowship in the works of God. Let us stand, praise his holy name.

Lord, we thank you. Great is thy faithfulness.

Great is thy faithfulness. Thank you for your mercies. Thank you for your love. Thank you for the way of the Most High God. Thank you for your word. It is a lamp, it is our light. It shows us the way that we must take. Help us to be blessed of God.

We hear the phrase used so, so lightly, Father... Be blessed. All we have to do is open up to the fifth chapter of Saint Matthew and see how to be blessed. Search our hearts through this word and see if we are blessed indeed of God. Hallelujah! You let your glorious sun shine on the good and the evil. Your mercies endure over all generations.

But Lord, you're searching, looking, seeking, longing for a people that will surely walk pleasing all together before you. Thy will be done. Thy kingdom come, you taught us to pray. As it is in heaven, so let it be done on earth. Lord, help us to love as you have taught us. Help us to be pitiful towards those, Lord, who despise us.

Help us to forgive. Help us to pray for our enemies. Help us to do it your way, Lord. Thy kingdom come in us that are called by your name. O most high God, we choose to follow your way. Thy kingdom come in a marvelous way.

Give your angels charge over us, directing us, bearing up our feet, keeping us from falling into self and into the snare of the devil. Bless us indeed to do your will. We trust you, O God. You are our Father. We glorify your name. We lift you up. We're thankful unto you. And we bless you. Bless your holy name.

O righteous Father, thank you for giving us freely of your Son, Jesus. Thank you, Jesus. Thank you, Lamb of God.

I love you today. Let everyone under the sound of this voice give you glory, give you praise, give you honor. Right the wrongs, heal the wounds, deliver in spirit. Fix it, Lord. Make it right in your sight. Loving Father, in Jesus' name we pray. Let your healing power flow right now.

Thy will be done. Those who are seeking your face even now, answer them speedily, Lord. Send help from on high. Grant them the power to do your will, the power to obey. Our help comes from the Lord, maker of heaven and earth. Hallelujah. In Jesus' name, we command it to be so from your mighty hand, our Father.

God be with you till we meet again, by the way of radio. Pray for us as we pray for you. Jesus is coming. We must be altogether pleasing in his sight. Amen.

LISTEN TO THE PODCAST

Listen to Evangelist Martha P. Davis today at your favorite podcast location. Just look for God's Holy Mountain Broadcast, or scan below:

www.ingramcontent.com/pod-product-compliance
Lightning Source LLC
Chambersburg PA
CBHW071716120626

46550CB00001B/264